Scott Foresman - Addison Wesley

MATH

Extend Your Thinking
Enrichment Masters

Grade 3

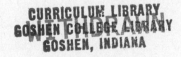
SF
AW

Scott Foresman - Addison Wesley

Editorial Offices: Menlo Park, California • Glenview, Illinois
Sales Offices: Reading, Massachusetts • Atlanta, Georgia • Glenview, Illinois
Carrollton, Texas • Menlo Park, California

http://www.sf.aw.com

ISBN 0-201-31262-X

Copyright © Addison Wesley Longman, Inc.

Printed in the United States of America

2 3 4 5 6 7 8 9 10 – BW – 02 01 00 99 98 97

Contents

Chapter 8: Using Geometry

Chapter 9: Multiplying and Dividing

Chapter 10: Fractions and Customary Linear Measurement

Chapter 11: Decimals and Metric Linear Measurement

Chapter 12: Measurement and Probability

Overview

Extend Your Thinking (Enrichment Masters) enhance student learning by actively involving students in different areas of mathematical reasoning. Activities often involve students in real-world situations, some of which may have more than one right answer. Thus, the masters motivate students to find alternate solutions to a given problem.

How to use

The *Extend Your Thinking* masters are designed so that the teacher can use them in many different ways.

  a. As a teaching tool to guide students in exploring a specific type of thinking skill. Making a transparency of the worksheet provides an excellent way to expedite this process as students work at their desks along with the teacher.

  b. As an enrichment worksheet that challenges and motivates students to hone their thinking skills.

  c. As independent or group work.

  d. As a homework assignment that encourages students to involve their parents in the educational process.

Description of the masters

The *Extend Your Thinking* masters consist of four types of motivating and challenging activities that focus on these four categories of higher-order thinking skills:

Patterns activities encourage students to develop skills in recognizing patterns that exist and are used in all facets of mathematics. Students are challenged to describe, extend, analyze, and generalize patterns. The study of patterns allows students to gain an appreciation for the inter-relatedness and beauty in the structure of mathematics.

These activities provide students with consistent exposure to *Patterns in Data, Patterns in Numbers, Patterns in Algebra,* and *Patterns in Geometry.*

Critical Thinking activities challenge students to examine and evaluate their own thinking about math. The problems and situations involve higher-order thinking skills such as analysis, synthesis, and evaluation. As students become more aware and more critical of their thinking, they learn to evaluate their own reasoning as they become better problem solvers.

The critical-thinking strategies students use include the following: *Classifying and Sorting, Ordering and Sequencing, Using Logic, Drawing Conclusions, Using Number Sense, Finding/Extending/Using Patterns, Making Generalizations, Reasoning with Graphs and Charts, Explaining Reasoning/Justifying Answers, Developing Alternatives, Evaluating Evidence and Conclusions,* and *Making and Testing Predictions.*

Visual Thinking activities focus on students' ability to perceive and mentally manipulate visual images. These types of activities are extremely important because visualization can often help develop students' critical thinking and problem solving skills.

Students are provided an opportunity to explore spatial perception as well as visual patterns using both two- and three-dimensional figures. Visual analogies provide practice in exploring logical reasoning. Many visual thinking pages integrate patterns and emphasize the integration of the mathematics strands.

Decision Making activities present enriching real-world situations that require students to make a decision. There are often no clearly right or clearly wrong answers. This gives the students the opportunity to make choices and consider alternatives.

You may wish to encourage students to use these steps as they make and evaluate their decisions.

Understand Encourage students to define the problem. They need to consider why a decision is needed, what goal they wish to meet, and what tools and techniques they can use to reach their decision.

Plan and Solve At this stage, students need to identify the options by isolating information that is relevant to the decision-making process. As they consider the advantages and disadvantages of each option, they are using skills that enable them to make an informed decision.

Make a Decision After students evaluate the data and consider both the positive and negative consequences of each possible decision, they decide which choice is best.

Present the Decision Students are often asked to explain why they feel a certain choice is more advantageous. Because different students may weigh each advantage and disadvantage differently, this concluding step can often lead to a useful, worthwhile class discussion.

Critical Thinking

The Ecology Club counted all the different kinds of trees in
Middletown Park. Here is their report:

Kind of Tree	Trees Counted
Oak	20
Maple	15
Willow	5
Pine	25
Birch	10

Your job is to make a pictograph of the report. Follow these steps.

1. Create a symbol.

2. Decide how many trees each symbol will represent.

3. Figure out how many symbols you need for each kind of
   tree in the pictograph.

4. Put each group of symbols where it belongs.

5. Make a key that shows what one symbol stands for.

6. Title your pictograph.

_____

Tree	Trees Counted
Oak	
Maple	
Willow	
Pine	
Birch	

Key: _____

Name _____

Critical Thinking

Your school's PTA took a survey about how much students read every day. They used the results of the survey to make this bar graph.

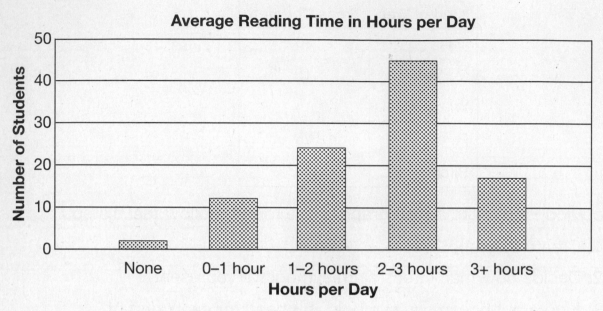

Use the bar graph to decide if each statement is true or false. If it is true, write True. If it is false, write False and explain why.

1. All students read every day.

_____

2. More students read for 1–2 hours per day than 2–3 hours per day.

_____

_____

3. The largest group of students reads for 2–3 hours per day.

_____

4. Most students read for 1–3 hours each day.

_____

5. 27 students read for more than 3 hours per day.

_____

Name _____

Visual Thinking

Ring the figures in each question that are exactly alike.

1.

2.

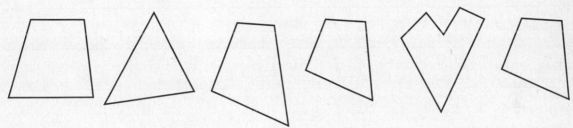

3.

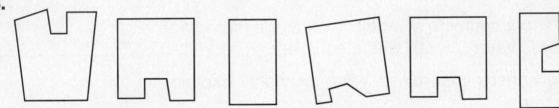

4.

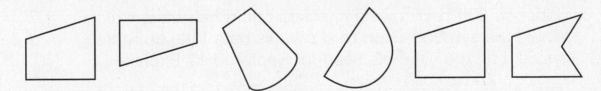

5.

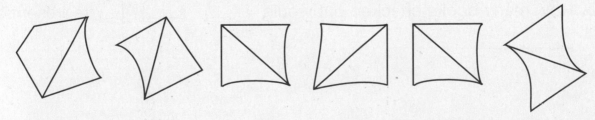

Critical Thinking

The librarian posted the following pictograph in your school library. It shows how many books were taken out of the library each month.

Use the pictograph to answer each question.

Books Checked Out of Our Library

Month	Books Checked Out
September	📖 📖 📖 📖 📖
October	📖 📖 📖 📖 📖
November	📖 📖 📖
December	📖 📖 📖 📖
January	📖 📖 📖 📖 📖 📖 📖

📖 = 100 books

1. Without counting symbols, look at the pictograph and guess which month was the busiest. _____

2. Now check your guess. Were you right? Explain.

   _____

   _____

3. Suppose 600 books were checked out in February. Would the symbols used to show this data take up more space than the symbols used for September? Explain.

   _____

4. How many books checked out would 📖 represent? _____

5. How many books checked out would 📖 📖 📖 represent? _____

   _____

Decision Making

Angela, Ralph, and Thale are playing together. They each brought their toy car collections, but they want everyone to have the same number to play with. What should they do?

Use the bar graph to help you decide.

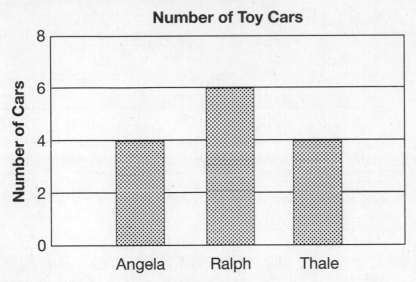

Number of Toy Cars

1. What can they do to make sure everyone has the same number of toy cars to play with?

_____

_____

2. How did you make this decision?

_____

_____

_____

3. a. What operation did you choose to find your solution?

_____

   b. Write the number sentence.

_____

4. Can you solve the problem without having to put any cars away?

_____

Patterns in Numbers

Complete each table. Then write the rule to explain changing
an **In** number to an **Out** number.

1.

In	1	3	4	5	6	7
Out	2	6	8			

Rule: _____

2.

In	1	3	5	8	4	10
Out	0	0	0			

Rule: _____

3.

In	1	2	3	4	5	6
Out	3	5	7			

Rule: _____

4.

In	12	20	35			
Out	15	23	38	41	57	62

Rule: _____

5.

In	12	20	35			
Out	8	16	31	37	45	67

Rule: _____

Visual Thinking

Circle the shape on the right that matches the shape on the left.

1.

2.

3.

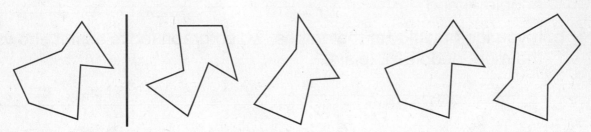

4.

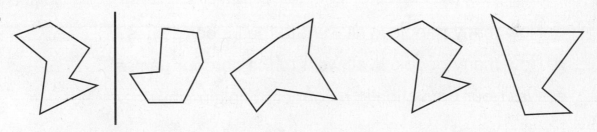

5.

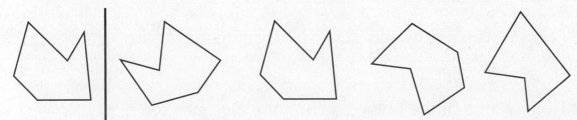

6.

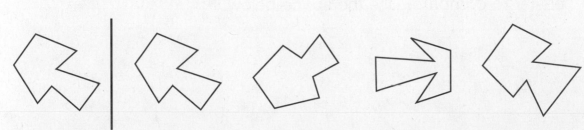

Critical Thinking

Use the pictograph to answer **1–2**.

Indoor Sports Attendance

Basketball	
Hockey	

= 10 people

Outdoor Sports Attendance

Softball	
Soccer	

= 20 people

1. a. Which two games do the most
people attend? _____

   b. If you look quickly at the graphs, which graph looks as if it shows
   the most people? Explain.

   _____

   _____

   c. How many people in all went to the indoor games? _____

   d. How many people in all went to the outdoor games? _____

   e. Was your prediction in **b** correct? Explain why or why not.

   _____

   _____

   _____

2. Redraw one of the graphs so that the 2 graphs are
easier to compare. Use the space below.

Visual Thinking

Circle the figure that shows the mirror image of the grid on the left.

Example:

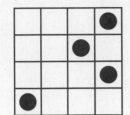

1.

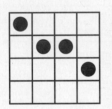 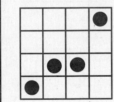 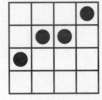 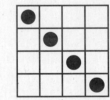 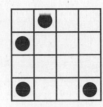

2.

 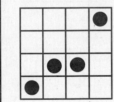   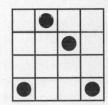

3.

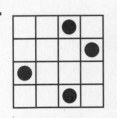 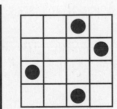 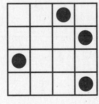 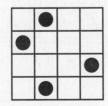 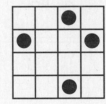

4.

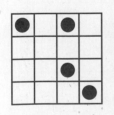 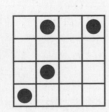 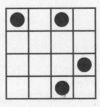 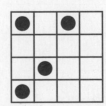 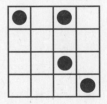

Decision Making

Your school is having a carnival. Your class wants to have a game booth to raise money for new sports equipment for the school. Your class has two choices.

Hoop Toss: Your class would set up prizes on stands and hoops for players to throw onto them. Prizes would cost $25.

Fish Bowl Toss: Your class would get some empty fish bowls and ping pong balls for players to throw into them. Prizes would cost $35.

Your class will charge $1.00 for each ticket to play a game.

To help you decide on a game, your class asked students what game they would like to play. This graph shows their votes.

Votes for Carnival Games

Hoop Toss	☺ ☺ ☺ ☺ ☺ ☺ ☺
Fish Bowl Toss	☺ ☺ ☺ ☺ ☺ ☺ ☺ ☺ ☺ ☺

☺ = 10 students

1. Suppose everybody who voted for the hoop toss game played it once. How much money would your class make on the hoop toss? _____

2. Suppose everybody who voted for the fish bowl toss played it once. How much money would your class make on the fish bowl toss? _____

3. Why would you not choose a hoop toss? Explain.

_____

4. Why would you not choose a fish bowl toss? Explain.

_____

_____

5. Which game would you choose to have? Explain.

_____

_____

Patterns in Numbers

Write numbers to complete the patterns. Then write the rule you used.

1. 2, 7, 12, 17, 22, 27, _____, _____, _____

Rule: _____

2. 5, 10, 20, 40, _____, _____, _____

Rule: _____

3. 2, 6, 10, 14, 18, 22, 24, _____, _____, _____

Rule: _____

4. 64, 32, 16, 8, _____, _____, _____

Rule: _____

5. 7, 8, 10, 13, _____, _____, _____

Rule: _____

6. 35, 34, 32, 29, 25, 20, _____, _____

Rule: _____

7. 100, 98, 94, 88, 80, _____, _____, _____

Rule: _____

8. 49, 40, 32, 25, _____, _____, _____

Rule: _____

9. 36, 30, 24, 18, _____, _____, _____

Rule: _____

10. 0, 9, 18, 27, _____, _____, _____

Rule: _____

Critical Thinking

Science The graph shows the speeds of insects in flight in order of speed from top to bottom.

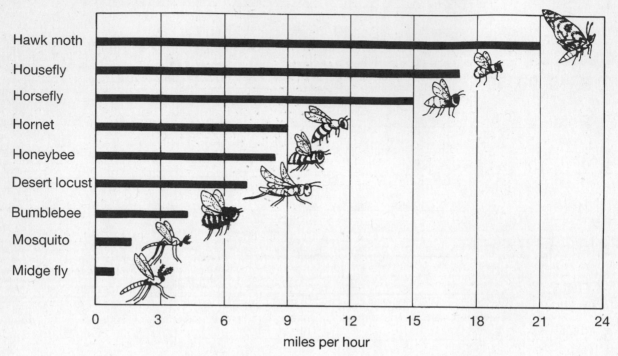

Hawk moth
Housefly
Horsefly
Hornet
Honeybee
Desert locust
Bumblebee
Mosquito
Midge fly

0   3   6   9   12   15   18   21   24
miles per hour

1. Which insect is the fastest? How fast does it fly? _____

_____

2. A dragonfly flies 18 miles per hour. Between which two insects would

   it be on the graph? _____

3. Which insect flies 6 miles per hour faster than the hornet? _____

4. In a race between a mosquito and a midge fly, which should win?

   Would the race be close? _____

5. Which flies faster, the housefly or the horsefly? How much faster?

_____

6. Small, light insects are slowed down by the air, which pushes against
   their wings and body. Which two insects are probably the smallest?

   Explain. _____

_____

Name _____

Patterns in Numbers

You can use place-value rules to make number patterns.
What are the next three numbers in each pattern? Complete
the rule.

1. 10, 20, 30, 40, _____, _____, _____

Rule: Increase the number in the _____ place by _____.

2. 5, 10, 15, 20, _____, _____, _____

Rule: Increase the number in the _____ place by _____.

3. 100, 200, 300, 400, _____, _____, _____

Rule: Increase the number in the _____ place by _____.

4. 35, 45, 55, 65, _____, _____, _____

Rule: Increase the number in the _____ place by _____.

5. 90, 80, 70, 60, _____, _____, _____

Rule: Decrease the number in the _____ place by _____.

6. 600, 500, 400, _____, _____, _____

Rule: Decrease the number in the _____ place by _____.

7. 35, 30, 25, _____, _____, _____

Rule: Decrease the number in the _____ place by _____.

8. 75, 65, 55, _____, _____, _____

Rule: Decrease the number in the _____ place by _____.

Critical Thinking

Use the clues to solve the puzzles.

1. My ones digit is 4. My tens digit is 3 plus my ones digit. My hundreds digit is 7 less than my thousands digit. My thousands digit is 8. What number am I? _____

2. My ones digit is 6. My tens digit is 1 plus my ones digit. My hundreds digit is 3 less than my tens digit. My thousands digit is 3 less than my hundreds digit. What number am I? _____

3. My ones digit is 1. Add 1 to my ones digit to get my tens digit. Add 1 to my tens digit to get my hundreds digit. Add 1 to my hundreds digit to get my thousands digit. What number am I? _____

4. My thousands digit is 3. My hundreds digit is $3 - 3$. My ones digit is 2. My tens digit is twice 2. What number am I? _____

5. The digit in my thousands place is 2. The digit in my ones place is 3 less than 10. The digits in the tens and hundreds places are the same. Together they add to 10. What number am I? _____

6. My ones digit and my thousands digit are the same. My tens digit is 2. My hundreds digit is 3 more than 2. My ones digit is $2 + 2$. What number am I? _____

7. The digit in my thousands place is 2. The digit in my hundreds place is 2 less than 2. My tens digit is 5. My ones digit is 1 less than 5. What number am I? _____

8. Write a place-value number riddle. Give it to a classmate to solve.

_____

_____

_____

_____

_____

_____

Name _____

Decision Making

Games Day is next week, and you're in charge of the games!
Here are some games you can play, the number of players you
need to make 2 teams, and the estimated time for each game.

> **a.** Basketball—10 players, 30 minutes
> **b.** Kickball—18 players, 15 minutes
> **c.** Indoor Soccer—10 players, 40 minutes
> **d.** Volleyball—12 players, 10 minutes

- A team may have more players than it needs, but not
  fewer. For example, you can have 12 players playing
  basketball, but not 8 players.

- Games Day lasts 4 hours.

Which games will you choose?

1. If all 4 games are played at the same time, how many
   players do you need?   _____

2. Choose any 2 games. How many players do you need?

   _____

   _____

   _____

3. Choose any 3 games. Which ones did you choose? How
   many players do you need?

   _____

   _____

   _____

4. Make a schedule for Games Day. Describe how you
   made your choices.

   _____

   _____

   _____

Critical Thinking

A swallowtail butterfly starts as an egg, then becomes a caterpillar. Next it enters the pupa stage, which it spends in a cocoon. Finally, it emerges as a bright yellow, red, and black butterfly!

What happens next? Use the clues to place the pictures in order from first to last.

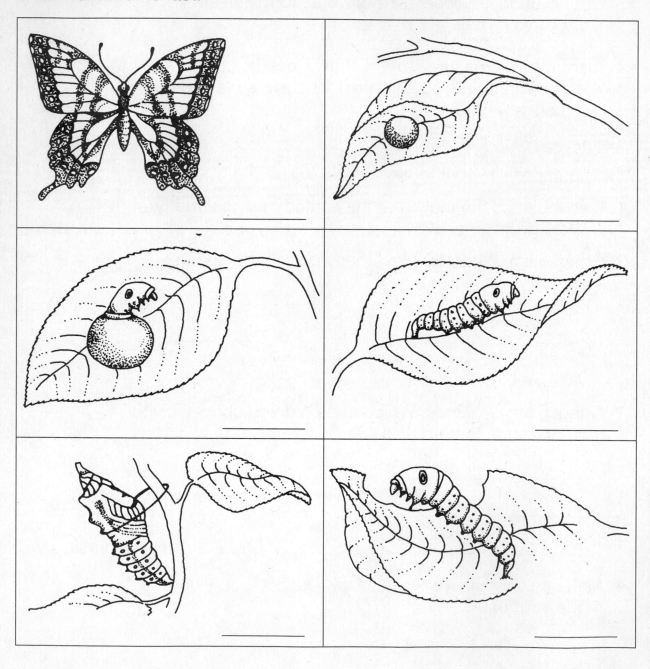

Name _____

Critical Thinking

Animals have different life spans. They live for different
lengths of time. The life spans of some animals are shown in
the bar graph.

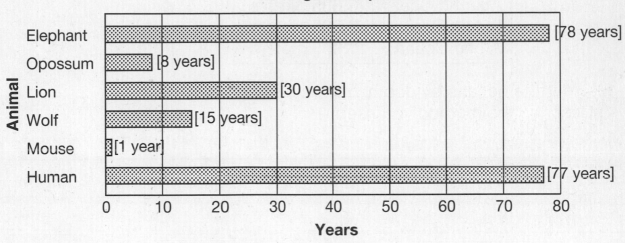

Average Life Spans

Elephant [78 years]
Opossum [8 years]
Lion [30 years]
Wolf [15 years]
Mouse [1 year]
Human [77 years]

Animal

0   10   20   30   40   50   60   70   80

Years

1. Which animal lives for the least number of years? How
   do you know?

   _____

   _____

2. Which animal is likely to live about as long as you? Explain.

   _____

   _____

3. Compare the life spans of these animals. Write a number
   sentence. Use $<$, $>$, or $=$.

   An elephant and a mouse: _____

   A lion and a wolf: _____

   A human and an opossum: _____

4. Suppose a friend tells you that his mouse is 10 years
   old. Would you believe him? Explain.

   _____

   _____

Critical Thinking

Use the information in this chart to answer the questions.

How Deep Is the Ocean?	
Pacific Ocean	4,280 meters
Atlantic Ocean	3,635 meters
Indian Ocean	3,905 meters
Arctic Ocean	1,055 meters

1. Order the oceans by depth, from least to greatest.
   Describe the method you used.

   _____

   _____

   _____

   _____

2. Which ocean do you think a submarine could get to the
   bottom of in the least amount of time? Why?

   _____

3. If it takes a submarine 1 hour to dive 1,000 meters,
   about how long do you think it would take to reach the
   bottom of the Pacific Ocean? Explain your reasoning.

   _____

   _____

4. A fish lives 3,500 meters below the surface of the water.
   In which oceans could this fish live?

   _____

Patterns in Numbers

The rules of rounding can be used to list numbers.

Write the numbers that follow each rule for **1** and **2**.

1. Rounded to the nearest ten, these numbers round to 50.

_____

2. Rounded to the nearest ten, these numbers round to 130.

_____

3. How many whole numbers rounded to the nearest ten round to 370? Give the least and greatest numbers.

_____

4. How would you write a rule for rounding to hundreds?

_____

_____

_____

Use your rule to answer **5** and **6**.

5. If you were rounding to the nearest hundred how many numbers do you think would round to 300? Give the least and greatest number. Explain your reasoning.

_____

_____

_____

6. How many numbers rounded to the nearest hundred round to 900? Give the least and greatest number.

_____

Visual Thinking

Read the secret code to find out these numbers.

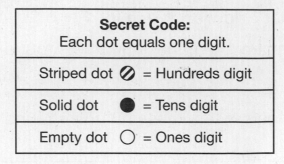

| **Secret Code:** |
| Each dot equals one digit. |
| Striped dot ⊘ = Hundreds digit |
| Solid dot ● = Tens digit |
| Empty dot ○ = Ones digit |

Example

⊘ ● ○
⊘ ● ○   242
  ●
  ●

1. ⊘ ● ○
⊘   ○
⊘   ○
     ○
     ○
     ○

2. ⊘ ●
    ●
    ●
    ●
    ●

Now try these!

3.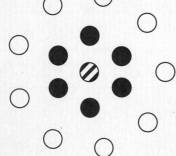

4.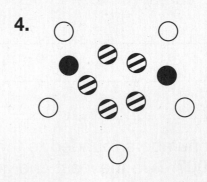

Write these numbers in the secret code.

5. 430

6. 913

Visual Thinking

These clocks only show the numbers 3, 6, 9, and 12. Look carefully at the hands to find the time. Write the time in numbers under each clock.

1. _____

2. _____

3. _____

4. _____

5. _____

6. _____

7. _____

8. _____

Critical Thinking

The Midtown Fire Department has one fire engine. One day, from 8:00 A.M. to 5:00 P.M., six calls came in at these times.

11:48 A.M.	8:28 A.M.
1:02 P.M.	4:47 P.M.
11:43 A.M.	3:18 P.M.

1. Put the calls in order, beginning with the earliest call.

   a. _____ b. _____ c. _____

   d. _____ e. _____ f. _____

2. What was the shortest amount of time between two calls?

   _____

3. What was the longest amount of time between two calls?

   _____

4. Which part of the shift was the busiest: 8:00 A.M.–11:00 A.M., 11:00 A.M.–2:00 P.M., or 2:00 P.M.–5:00 P.M.?

   _____

5. If you had your choice of shifts, which shift would you like to work? Explain.

   _____

   _____

6. Based on the data above, does the Midtown Fire Department need more than one fire truck? Explain your reasoning.

   _____

Name _____

Visual Thinking

Lee got a new wristwatch. There's one problem. It doesn't have any numbers on it! Look at the hands and the marks on the clocks. Write the times in numbers under each watch.

1. _____

2. _____

3. _____

4. _____

5. _____

6. _____

7. _____

8. _____

Decision Making

Your best friend is coming on Saturday for a visit. She will arrive at 1:00 P.M. You must be ready to take her home at 3:10 P.M. You want to do something special, so you look in the newspaper. Here's what you find:

• **Storytelling Time** begins at the library at 2:30 P.M. It will last for 45 minutes.

• **Student Concerts** begin downtown at 12:30 P.M., 2:00 P.M., and 4:30 P.M. They each last one hour.

• **A movie** begins at 1:45 P.M. and runs for two hours and ten minutes.

• **A karate demonstration** begins at your school at 1:30. It will last for an hour and a half.

1. What time will the Storytelling Time end? _____

2. What time will each concert end?

_____, _____, and _____.

3. What time will the movie end? _____

4. What time will the karate demonstration end? _____

5. Which activities will you and your friend have time for?

_____

_____

6. Which activity would you choose? Why?

_____

_____

Critical Thinking

Your class wants to add some new holidays to the calendar!

Use the calendar below to find the date for each holiday listed below. Write the date next to each holiday's name.

June

Sun.	Mon.	Tues.	Wed.	Thur.	Fri.	Sat.
1	2	3	4	5	6	7
8	9	10	11	12	13	14
15	16	17	18	19	20	21
22	23	24	25	26	27	28
29	30					

July

Sun.	Mon.	Tues.	Wed.	Thur.	Fri.	Sat.
		1	2	3	4	5
6	7	8	9	10	11	12
13	14	15	16	17	18	19
20	21	22	23	24	25	26
27	28	29	30	31		

August

Sun.	Mon.	Tues.	Wed.	Thur.	Fri.	Sat.
					1	2
3	4	5	6	7	8	9
10	11	12	13	14	15	16
17	18	19	20	21	22	23
24 / 31	25	26	27	28	29	30

September

Sun.	Mon.	Tues.	Wed.	Thur.	Fri.	Sat.
	1	2	3	4	5	6
7	8	9	10	11	12	13
14	15	16	17	18	19	20
21	22	23	24	25	26	27
28	29	30				

October

Sun.	Mon.	Tues.	Wed.	Thur.	Fri.	Sat.
			1	2	3	4
5	6	7	8	9	10	11
12	13	14	15	16	17	18
19	20	21	22	23	24	25
26	27	28	29	30	31	

November

Sun.	Mon.	Tues.	Wed.	Thur.	Fri.	Sat.
						1
2	3	4	5	6	7	8
9	10	11	12	13	14	15
16	17	18	19	20	21	22
23 / 30	24	25	26	27	28	29

1. **Pet Day:** the first Friday in June: _____

2. **Best Friend Day:** the third Monday in October: _____

3. **Pizza Day:** the fourth Tuesday in July: _____

4. **Pen-Pal Day:** the second Wednesday in September: _____

5. **Exercise Day:** the third Friday in November: _____

6. **Hat Day:** the first Thursday in August: _____

7. **Your Own Holiday:** the fifth Monday in September: _____

Decision Making

You're in charge of making a schedule for the Pet Club meeting. Here is the list of activities for the meeting.

• Announcements _____

• Dr. Evans talks about "Your Pets' Teeth." __20 minutes__

• Roberto shows his pet guinea pig. _____

• Jody shows her pet iguana. _____

• Samantha shows her pet tarantula. _____

The meeting will begin at 4:00 P.M. and end at 5:00 P.M.

1. How much time do you have? _____

2. Dr. Evans, the vet, needs 20 minutes. How much time will each of the other activities take? Write your estimates next to each activity.

_____

_____

3. Make a schedule for the meeting. Write it in the chart.

Pet Club Meeting	
Time	Activity
P.M.	
P.M.	
P.M.	
P.M.	
P.M.	

4. Compare your schedule with one or two friends. How are the schedules different?

_____

_____

Patterns in Algebra

Basic facts and place-value patterns can help you add greater numbers.

Use patterns to help you fill in the blanks.

1. 60 + _____ = 130

2. _____ + 30 = 120

3. 40 + 60 = _____

4. 60 + _____ = 110

5. _____ + 700 = 1,300

6. 50 + _____ = 120

7. 900 + _____ = 1,200

8. _____ + 30 = 90

9. _____ + 300 = 700

10. _____ + 600 = 1,000

11. 700 + 900 = _____

12. 600 + 500 = _____

13. 500 + 700 = _____

14. 40 + 30 = _____

15. 600 + _____ = 900

16. _____ + 90 = 160

17. 400 + _____ = 900

18. 70 + _____ = 140

19. _____ + 80 = 150

20. _____ + 300 = 500

21. 600 + _____ = 1,400

22. 90 + _____ = 180

23. 50 + _____ = 130

24. 20 + _____ = 110

25. _____ + 400 = 1,200

26. 700 + _____ = 900

27. _____ + 400 = 1,100

28. _____ + 900 = 1,500

29. 300 + _____ = 1,100

30. _____ + 700 = 900

31. _____ + 400 = 1,000

32. _____ + 900 = 1,800

Critical Thinking

1	2	3	4	5	6	7	8	9	10
11	12	13	14	15	16	17	18	19	20
21	22	23	24	25	26	27	28	29	30
31	32	33	34	35	36	37	38	39	40
41	42	43	44	45	46	47	48	49	50
51	52	53	54	55	56	57	58	59	60
61	62	63	64	65	66	67	68	69	70
71	72	73	74	75	76	77	78	79	80
81	82	83	84	85	86	87	88	89	90
91	92	93	94	95	96	97	98	99	100

Beth and Seth are playing a game. They each put a counter on the hundreds chart.

1. Beth says, "If you go over 2 spaces to the right and up 3 rows from my number, you will be at 27. What is my number?" Explain your reasoning.

   _____

   _____

2. Seth says, "If you go over 3 spaces to the left and down 2 rows from my number, you will be at 85. What is my number?" Explain your reasoning.

   _____

3. Beth says, "If you go over to the right 4 spaces from my number, you will move into the 70's row for the last 2 spaces. What is my number?" Explain your reasoning.

   _____

   _____

4. Seth says, "From my number, go up 2 rows and over to the left 3 spaces. You will be at 39. What's my number?" Explain your reasoning.

   _____

   _____

Visual Thinking

Choose the shape that can be added to the first shape to
make the second shape. Circle your choice.

1. 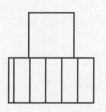 |

2. |

3. 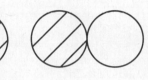 |

4.  |

5. |

6. 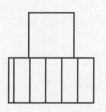 |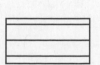

Decision Making

Your Little League team wants to buy
new uniforms and new equipment.
There are 18 players on your team.
Your coach has created a list with
packages of different items and their
costs. However, the team will only
buy 2 packages on the list.

Packages of:	Total Cost
18 baseball caps	$63
2 dozen t-shirts	$76
18 pairs of socks	$24
18 sweatshirts	$81
6 baseballs	$39
4 bats	$45

1. a. What are the 2 most expensive packages on the list?

_____

b. About how much is their total cost? _____

2. a. Which 2 packages on the list could be purchased for
about $65?

_____

b. What are their total costs? _____

3. There are other things besides cost to consider when
making your decision. What questions would you ask to
help you choose the two packages? List two questions
below.

Question 1: _____

Question 2: _____

4. Do you have enough information to make a decision?
Explain.

_____

_____

_____

5. Choose two packages to buy. Tell how much they cost
and why you chose them.

_____

_____

Critical Thinking

Here is a list of some of the tallest buildings in Cleveland, Ohio.

Tallest Buildings in Cleveland, Ohio	
Building	**Number of Stories**
Society Center	57
Terminal Tower	52
Bank One Center	28
Federal Building	32
J.A. Rhodes Tower	23
Ohio-Bell	22

1. **a.** What is the total number of stories in the Society Center and the J.A. Rhodes Tower? _____

   b. How did you find the answer?

   _____

   c. How can you check your answer?

   _____

2. Suppose the owners of the Ohio-Bell building decide to add 19 stories to the building and the owners of the Bank One Center decide to add 24 stories to their building. After construction, which building will be the tallest in the list? Explain.

   _____

   _____

   _____

   _____

Critical Thinking

Joanie writes in a journal where she keeps track of how much she reads each day for different subjects in school and for fun.

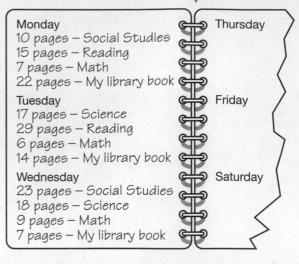

Monday
10 pages – Social Studies
15 pages – Reading
7 pages – Math
22 pages – My library book

Tuesday
17 pages – Science
29 pages – Reading
6 pages – Math
14 pages – My library book

Wednesday
23 pages – Social Studies
18 pages – Science
9 pages – Math
7 pages – My library book

Thursday

Friday

Saturday

1. How many total pages has Joanie read for science class?

_____

2. How many pages did Joanie read in all on Monday?

_____

3. What is the total number of pages Joanie read for social studies?

_____

4. Joanie has to read 40 pages for science this week.

a. How many more pages does Joanie have to read? _____

b. What strategy did you use to solve the problem? _____

_____

c. How many pages for science could Joanie read on Thursday and

Friday to meet her goal? _____

_____

5. On Sunday, Joanie had 100 pages left to read in her library book.

a. How many pages does she have to read now? _____

b. The library book is due on Saturday. How many pages could Joanie read on Thursday and Friday so that she completes the book?

_____

_____

Visual Thinking

A group of students found this paper in the gym. It shows addition problems written in code. The table gives some information about the code. Use the table to crack the code. Then solve the problems. Be sure to use the code to give your answers!

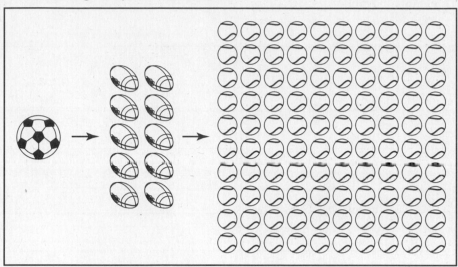

Write a number sentence and find the sum for each.

1. 🍂🍂🍂🍂🏉🏉🏉🏉ooo and 🍂🍂🏉🏉oooooo

_____

2. 🍂🍂🍂🍂🍂🏉🏉🏉ooo and 🍂🍂🍂🍂🏉🏉🏉🏉🏉🏉oooo

_____

3. 🍂🏉🏉🏉🏉ooooo and 🍂🍂🍂🍂🏉🏉ooo
🍂🏉🏉🏉oooo   🍂🍂

_____

4. 🍂🍂🍂🏉oo and 🍂🍂🍂🍂ooooooooo

_____

Patterns in Numbers

What are the next three numbers? Tell what rule was used to make the pattern.

1. 1,550; 1,650; 1,750; 1,850; _____; _____; _____

Rule: _____

2. 3,120; 3,270; 3,420; 3,570; _____; _____; _____

Rule: _____

3. 4,600; 5,200; 5,900; 6,700; _____; _____; _____

Rule: _____

4. 149; 298; 596; 1,192; _____; _____; _____

Rule: _____

5. 452; 563; 785; 1,118; _____; _____; _____

Rule: _____

_____

6. 1,239; 1,564; 1,989; 2,514; _____; _____; _____

Rule: _____

7. 234; 334; 534; 834; _____; _____; _____

Rule: _____

Name _____

Decision Making

The Science Club has collected 192 rock samples. The rocks need to be classified according to similar traits. Club members observed the rocks. They made this chart.

Trait	Number of Rocks
Light colored, round edges, leaves a streak	22
Dark colored, round edges, leaves a streak	18
Light colored, sharp edges, leaves a streak	17
Dark colored, sharp edges, leaves a streak	29
Light colored, round edges, no streak	16
Dark colored, round edges, no streak	44
Light colored, sharp edges, no streak	20
Dark colored, sharp edges, no streak	26

Club members have decided to use egg cartons to hold their rocks. They can place up to 12 rocks in each egg carton.

1. The club could classify the rocks as either light or dark colored. If they use this plan, how many egg cartons would be needed to hold the light colored rocks? The dark colored?

_____

2. The club could classify the rocks as those with round edges leaving a streak, with round edges leaving no streak, with sharp edges leaving a streak, and with sharp edges leaving no streak. If they use this plan, how many egg cartons would be needed to hold each group?

_____

_____

3. How do you think the club should classify the rocks? Create a classification system for the club. Describe it below.

_____

_____

Critical Thinking

1.

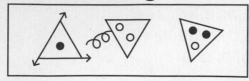 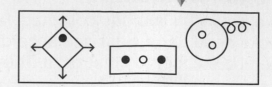

These are clanks.   These are not clanks.

How are all clanks alike?

2.

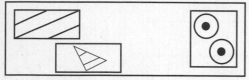 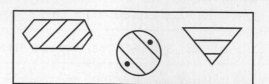

These are kwumps.   These are not kwumps.

How are all kwumps alike?

3.

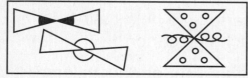 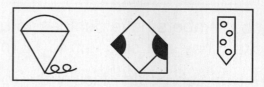

These are brips.   These are not brips.

How are all brips alike?

4.

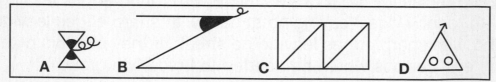

Which of these is a

a. clank? _____   **b.** kwump? _____   **c.** brip? _____

5. In the box below, draw a clank, kwump, and brip.

clank	kwump	brip

Patterns in Numbers

Use mental math to find the next three numbers in each pattern.
Tell what rule was used to make the pattern.

1. 11, 21, 31, 41, _____, _____, _____

Rule: _____

2. 25, 38, 51, 64, _____, _____, _____

Rule: _____

3. 17, 33, 49, 65, _____, _____, _____

Rule: _____

4. 24, 44, 64, 84, _____, _____, _____

Rule: _____

5. 11, 20, 29, 38, _____, _____, _____

Rule: _____

6. 11, 32, 53, 74, _____, _____, _____

Rule: _____

7. 48, 64, 80, 96, _____, _____, _____

Rule: _____

8. 16, 58, 100, _____, _____, _____

Rule: _____

Name _____

Critical Thinking

Three coins used in the United States during the 1800's are shown below. The value of each of these coins was greater than $1.00!

$10  $20  $50

Eagle   Double Eagle $50 Gold Piece

1. How many eagles equals one $50 gold piece? How do you know?

_____

2.

What is the total value of

these coins? _____

3.

What is the total value of

these coins? _____

4. Describe how you found the total value of the coins in **2** and **3**.

_____

5. Find four ways to make $100.00.

_____

_____

6. Each of these coins was replaced with paper money. Why do you think this change was made?

_____

Critical Thinking

Your class is holding a coin collection display. Three
students bring in their collections. You have 4 quarters,
7 dimes, 5 nickels, and 10 pennies. José has 6 quarters,
5 dimes, 3 nickels, and 7 pennies. Margaret has 3 quarters,
4 dimes, 8 nickels, and 10 pennies.

1. How many coins are there in each collection?

    a. yours _____   **b.** José's _____   **c.** Margaret's _____

2. What is the total value of each collection?

    a. yours _____   **b.** José's _____   **c.** Margaret's _____

3. Here is a bar graph of your coin collection. Add bars to
the graph to show José's and Margaret's coin collections.

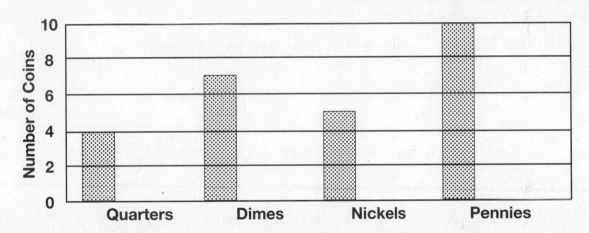

4. Is the coin collection with the greatest number of coins
also the one with greatest value? Why?

_____

_____

_____

Critical Thinking

Your music class is having a bake sale to raise money for new instruments. You are the cashier. You start with 3 one-dollar bills, 12 quarters, 10 dimes, 10 nickels, and 15 pennies in the cash register.

Price List	
oatmeal cookie	$0.76
apple pie	$3.82
muffin	$1.39
strawberry shortcake	$2.99

1. How much money is in the cash register? _____

2. Jim is first in line. He buys a muffin with $5.00.

   a. How much change will you give Jim? _____

   b. Which bills and coins will you use?

   _____

   c. Which bills and coins are in the cash register now?

   _____

   _____

2. Lucia is second in line. She buys an apple pie with $5.00.

   a. How much change will you give her? _____

   b. Which bills and coins will you use? (Remember, you have different bills and coins in the cash register now!)

   _____

   c. Which bills and coins are in the cash register now?

   _____

   _____

3. If a customer gave you a five-dollar bill to pay for a piece of strawberry shortcake, would you be able to make change? Explain.

   _____

   _____

Patterns in Numbers

Continue each pattern. Write the next three numbers using
dollars and cents or just cents. Then write the rule.

1. 12¢, 22¢, 32¢, 42¢, _____, _____, _____

Rule: _____

2. $0.55, $0.80, $1.05, $1.30, _____, _____, _____

Rule: _____

3. 36¢, 42¢, 48¢, 54¢, _____, _____, _____

Rule: _____

4. $0.89, $2.14, $3.39, $4.64, _____, _____, _____

Rule: _____

5. 109¢, 251¢, 393¢, 535¢, _____, _____, _____

Rule: _____

6. $1.99, $2.07, $2.15, $2.23, _____, _____, _____

Rule: _____

7. $0.12, $1.13, $2.14, $3.15, _____, _____, _____

Rule: _____

8. 15¢, 57¢, 99¢, 141¢, _____, _____, _____

Rule: _____

9. $0.03, $2.02, $4.01, $6.00, _____, _____, _____

Rule: _____

10. 5¢, 22¢, 39¢, 56¢, _____, _____, _____

Rule: _____

Decision Making

On Saturday you are going to spend the day with your
5-year-old sister and your aunt. You plan to choose a fun
place to visit. Together you have $18.00 to spend.

1. How much will it cost for all of you to go to the Paintings
   Museum? First estimate by using front-end estimation.
   Then add to find the exact sum.

   _____

2. How much will it cost for all of you to go to the Outdoor
   Sculpture Park? First estimate. Then find the exact sum.

   _____

3. How much will it cost for all of you to go to the movies?
   First estimate, then find the exact sum.

   _____

4. Think about what you will see at each place. Rank the
   places from the place you would most like to visit to the
   place you would least like to visit.

   _____

5. Which place will you choose to visit? Why?

   _____

   _____

   _____

Decision Making

You've just given your dog a bath in your bathtub and it made quite a mess. You are going to the hardware store to buy supplies to clean the bathroom. You have $15.00 to spend. You find a mop for $6.63, liquid soap for $1.89, a broom for $4.12, paper towels for $1.19 and a pack of sponges for $3.27.

1. List three items you can purchase with $15.00.

   _____

   _____

2. Which two items do you think would be the most important to buy? Why?

   _____

   _____

3. Which two items do you think would be the least important to buy? Why?

   _____

   _____

4. Which items would you purchase to clean the bathroom without going over $15.00?

   _____

   _____

5. What is the total cost of your purchase?

   _____

6. How much change would you receive from $15.00?

   _____

7. Describe how you made your choices.

   _____

Visual Thinking

Circle the animal in each row that is different.

1.

2.

3.

4.

5.

Critical Thinking

A stationery store is planning to have a grand opening. In order to attract customers, the store is going to give away free pencils.

The store manager needs to keep track of how many pencils are given out, so that she can get more when needed. She starts off with 1,000 pencils in stock. Every hour, she checks her supply.

Use subtraction and addition patterns to complete the table.

Each picture of a pencil on the chart represents 100 pencils. Write your answers in numbers.

	Time	Pencils Given Away	Pencils Re-Stocked	Pencils in Stock
1.	9:00 A.M.	none	none	1,000
2.	10:00 A.M.	🖉🖉🖉	none	
3.	11:00 A.M.	🖉🖉🖉🖉🖉	none	
4.	12:00 A.M.	🖉🖉	🖉🖉🖉🖉🖉	
5.	1:00 P.M.	🖉🖉🖉🖉	🖉🖉🖉🖉🖉🖉	
6.	2:00 P.M.	🖉🖉🖉	🖉🖉	
7.	3:00 P.M.	🖉🖉	none	
8.	4:00 P.M.	🖉	🖉🖉	
9.	5:00 P.M.	none	none	

10. How many pencils did the manager give away in total?

_____

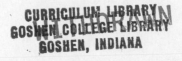

Patterns in Numbers

All of the third-graders at the Dorset Elementary School are
working hard to raise money for new equipment for the
school playground. The Community Parks Committee has
volunteered to donate $100 for every $10 that the students
raise. The goal is to raise $3,000. Use the chart below to see
how they meet their goal.

	Week 1	Week 2	Week 3
Money Raised by Students	$40	$250	$60
Contribution			

1. In which week do the students meet their goal? _____

2. What is the total contribution made by the Parks Committee?

_____

3. How much money do the students raise on their own?

_____

4. How much money was raised all together? _____

5. Suppose the students raised $100 in the second week.
Create a new chart that shows how the students could
meet their goal in 5 weeks.

Patterns in Numbers

A	B	C	D	E

 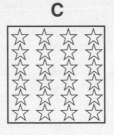 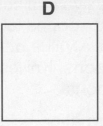 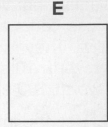

1. How many stars should be in box D
   in order to continue the pattern?   _____

2. About how many stars should be in box E?   _____

3. What is the exact amount of stars that
   should be in box E?   _____

4. Explain the rule for this pattern.

   _____

Make a list or choose any strategy to answer the questions.

5. **a.** If the pattern continued which box would be
   the first to have more than 1,000 stars?   _____

   b. Which box would be the first to have more
   than 5,000 stars?   _____

6. Fill in boxes D and E with the correct number
   of triangles.

A	B	C	D	E

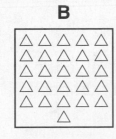 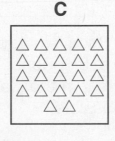  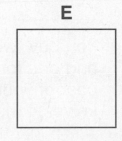

7. Explain the rule for this pattern.

   _____

Critical Thinking

Imagine that you live in a country where the people use
knives, forks and spoons for money! Spoons have the least
value. They have a value of 1. Forks are worth more. They
are worth 10 spoons. Knives have the most value. Each knife
is worth 100 spoons.

1. Use the information below to figure out the amount shown.

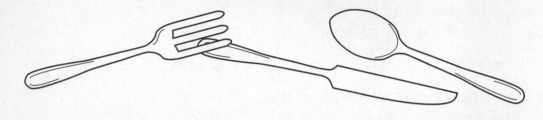

_____ spoons

2. Suppose you are shopping in this country. You want to
buy something that costs 4 knives, 6 forks. You have
only 3 knives and 17 forks.

   a. How can you make your purchase? Explain.

   _____

   b. How much will you have left? _____

3. You want to buy something for 1 knife, 6 forks, 4
spoons. You give the seller 2 knives. What will your
change be?

   _____

4. You buy two items; one for 3 knives, 4 forks, 7 spoons,
and one for 4 knives, 7 forks, 8 spoons. What is the total
cost of your purchase? Write it in the least number of
knives, forks and spoons possible.

   _____

5. Write your own problem using knives, forks and spoons
as money. Share it with a friend.

   _____

   _____

Critical Thinking

The amount of time animals need to carry their young until they are born can vary greatly. Use the information below to answer the questions.

Cats	63 days	Mice	20 days
Dogs	61 days	Rabbits	31 days
Foxes	52 days	Squirrels	44 days
Guinea Pigs	68 days	Wolves	63 days
Kangaroos	42 days		

1. Would you say a rabbit needs about a month for its young to be born? Explain.

_____

2. Would you say a kangaroo and a squirrel need about the same amount of time? Explain.

_____

_____

3. About how many months do cats and wolves need? Explain.

_____

_____

4. List the animals that need more than one month but less than 2 months.

_____

5. List the animals that need about 6 weeks. Explain.

_____

6. Which animal needs only about 3 weeks? Explain.

_____

_____

Critical Thinking

Lizette wants to exchange her coins, but she doesn't have enough. Write the amount of money she needs to exchange for the amount shown.

1. Lizette needs _____ to exchange the coins for 25¢.

2. Lizette needs _____ to exchange the coins for 50¢.

3. Lizette needs _____ to exchange the coins for $1.00.

4. Lizette needs _____ to exchange the coins for $1.00.

5. Lizette needs _____ to exchange the coins for $2.00.

6. Lizette needs _____ to exchange the coins for $5.00.

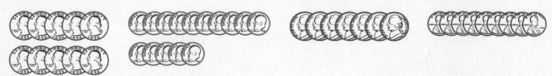

7. Describe how you found the amount of money Lizette needed.

_____

_____

Patterns in Numbers

Write the next 3 numbers in each pattern. Then write the rule
you used to complete the pattern.

1. 190, 180, 170, _____, _____, _____

Rule: _____

2. 240, 220, 200, _____, _____, _____

Rule: _____

3. 10, 40, 70, _____, _____, _____

Rule: _____

4. 50, 100, 150, _____, _____, _____

Rule: _____

5. 195, 180, 165, _____, _____, _____

Rule: _____

6. 178, 169, 160, _____, _____, _____

Rule: _____

7. 204, 191, 178, _____, _____, _____

Rule: _____

8. 107, 142, 177, _____, _____, _____

Rule: _____

9. 935, 811, 687, _____, _____, _____

Rule: _____

10. 849, 695, 541, _____, _____, _____

Rule: _____

11. 500, 467, 434, 401, _____, _____, _____

Rule: _____

Visual Thinking

Look at the two shapes on the left in each row. Imagine that the smaller shape is cut out of the larger shape. Circle the shape on the right that shows the remaining cut shape.

1.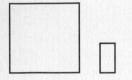

     a.   **b.**   **c.**   **d.**

2.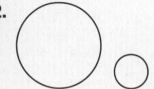

     a.   **b.**   **c.**   **d.**

3.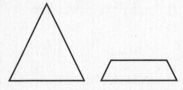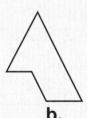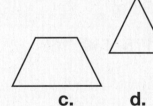

     a.   **b.**   **c.**   **d.**

4.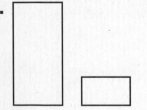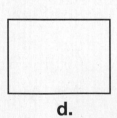

     a.   **b.**   **c.**   **d.**

5.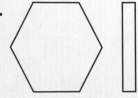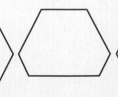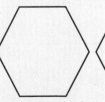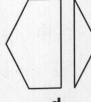

     a.   **b.**   **c.**   **d.**

Name _____

Critical Thinking

North America has many different rivers running through it. In fact, rivers can be longer than some states! Here are some rivers which run through North America. Use the table to answer the questions.

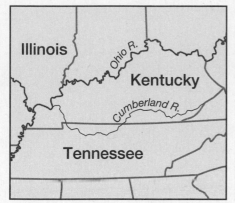

River	Where it Starts	Length in Miles
Cumberland	Kentucky	720
Yellowstone	Wyoming	692
Ohio-Allegheny	Pennsylvania	981
Tombigbee	Mississippi	525
Liard	Alaska	693
Brazos	Texas	923
Sacramento	California	377

1. What is the difference in length between the longest river

   and the shortest river? _____

2. If you drive straight across from one side of Colorado to the other, you will have driven approximately 385 miles. How much longer would you have to drive to cover the entire length of the Brazos river? Explain.

_____

_____

3. Felicia likes to go white-water rafting on rivers across North America. If she travels 120 miles each day, how many days will it take her to raft the entire length of the Cumberland river?

   a. Make a table at the right to help you find the answer. Use the headings "Number of days" and "Number of miles" in each column.

   b. How many days will it take Felicia to raft the Cumberland river?

   _____

Rafting the Cumberland	

Decision Making

Lynn's goal for her summer vacation is to read a total of
500 pages. So far, she has read 383 pages. She has time
to read one more book before the end of the summer. She
has narrowed down her book choices to 3 books from her
local library.

Book A: *The Wonderful World of Bugs*—134 pages

Book B: *The Summer Dance*—122 pages

Book C: *Scary Tales of Lore*—140 pages

1. How many more pages does Lynn need to read to reach

her goal of 500 pages? _____

2. Will each of the books allow Lynn to reach her goal?
Write yes or no.

Book A _____   Book B _____   Book C _____

3. How many pages over or under her goal will Lynn read
for each book choice?

Book A _____   Book B _____   Book C _____

4. Look at each book's title. What do you think each book
is about? Explain.

Book A: _____

Book B: _____

Book C: _____

5. Which book do you think Lynn should read? Why?

_____

_____

_____

Patterns in Numbers

Use patterns to help you fill in the blanks.

1. 7 − 4 = _____

    70 − 40 = _____

    700 − 400 = _____

    7,000 − 4,000 = _____

2. _____ − 200 = 600

    8 − _____ = 6

    80 − 20 = _____

    _____ − 2,000 = 6,000

3. 9 − 3 = _____

    90 − _____ = 60

    900 − 300 = _____

    _____ − 3,000 = 6,000

4. 1,200 − _____ = 700

    120 − 50 = _____

    _____ − 5 = 7

5. 150 − 80 = _____

    15 − _____ = 7

    _____ − 800 = 700

6. 23 − 14 = _____

    230 − _____ = 90

    _____ − 1,400 = 900

7. 60 − _____ = 50

    6,000 − 1,000 = _____

    _____ − 100 = 500

    6 − 1 = _____

8. 340 − 170 = _____

    3,400 − 1,700 = _____

    _____ − 17 = 17

    34,000 − _____ = 17,000

Complete the patterns. Write the rule for each.

9. 6,543; 6,366; 6,189; _____; _____

    Rule: _____

10. 5,709; 5,654; _____; _____; _____

    Rule: _____

Critical Thinking

Mrs. Lyons baked 85 loaves of bread for the school bake sale. The sale ran for 3 days. On the first day, Monday, 35 loaves were sold. At the end of the second day, there were 25 left. On the third day, 14 more were sold. Mrs. Lyons will receive a prize from the bake sale committee if she sells at least 70 loaves.

1. How many loaves were sold on:

   a. Monday? _____

   b. Tuesday? _____

   c. Wednesday? _____

2. How many loaves did Mrs. Lyons sell all together? _____

3. Did Mrs. Lyons sell all the bread she made? _____

4. Will Mrs. Lyons win the prize? _____

5. Did Mrs. Lyons have to sell any bread at all on Wednesday in order to win the prize? Explain.

_____

6. If Mrs. Lyons had sold only 20 loaves on Tuesday, would she have sold enough to win the prize? How do you know?

_____

_____

7. Mrs. Lyons decided to sell bread on Thursday until she sold all that was left. How many loaves does Mrs. Lyons have to sell?

_____

8. Mrs. Lyons baked muffins for the next bake sale, which ran for 4 days. If she needed to sell 75 muffins to win a prize and she sold about the same number each day, about how many would she have to sell each day?

_____

Decision Making

Roberto, Michael and Stephanie are planning a route for a bike-a-thon. The bike ride will start and finish at the park.

Use the map and the following information to plan a route.

- The route should be 15 to 20 blocks long.
- The route must pass the library, the school and the bookstore.
- Bikers are not allowed to ride on the same block more than once.

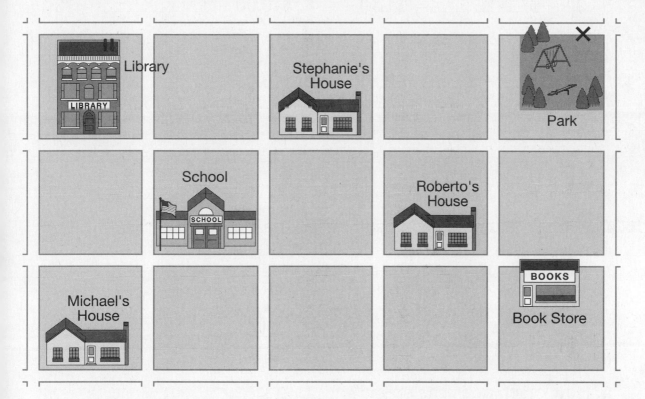

1. Draw your route on the map. Explain why you chose the route you did.

   _____

   _____

2. If Roberto wanted to ride from home to Michael's house and pass by Stephanie's house on the way, what are the least number of blocks he would have to ride?

   _____

3. Using a different colored pencil, draw a route around as many blocks as you can without riding on the same stretch of road twice.

Critical Thinking

Find the missing digits.

1. $15 – $_____ = $9

2. $27 – $_____ = $13

3. $_____ – $26 = $32

4. $_____ – $47 = $54

5. $37 – $_____ = $24

6. $_____ – $81 = $10

7. $4.32 – $_____ = $1.19

8. $10.00 – $_____ = $3.16

9. $_____ – $1.21 = $7.62

10. $_____ – $6.21 = $13.61

11. $_____ – $8.42 = $20.00

12. $15.00 – $_____ = $9.79

13.
```
  $ 4 . □9
-   1 . 8 □
  $ □ . 6 5
```

14.
```
  $ 2 □ . □8
-     6 . 4 □
  $ □ 4 . 2 9
```

15.
```
  $ 1 5 . □7
-     9 . 4 □
  $   □ . 7 6
```

16. Describe the method you used to find the missing digits.

_____

_____

17. Karen has $10. She buys one item for $1.74 and another for $2.29.

    a. How much does she spend? _____

    b. How much change will she get from a $5 bill?

    _____

    c. Does she have enough money left for 3 items costing $2.03 each? Explain.

    _____

Visual Thinking

Look for a pattern. Draw the fourth figure to complete the pattern.

1.

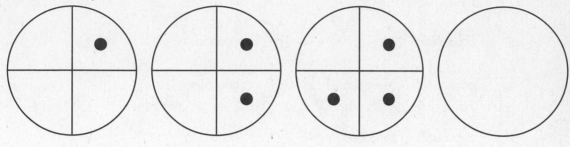

2.

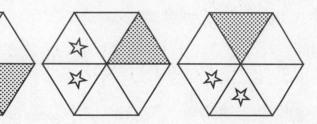
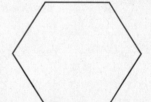

3.

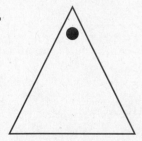
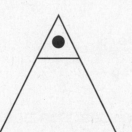
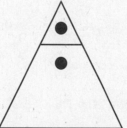
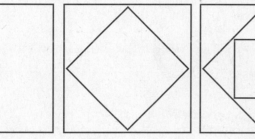

4.

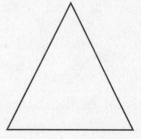

5.

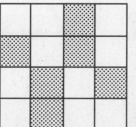
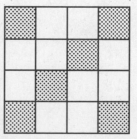

Visual Thinking

Continue the pattern. Draw the next two sets of beads.

1.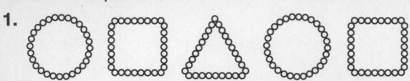

2.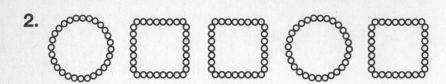

3.

4.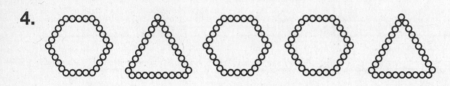

5.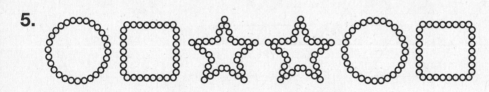

6.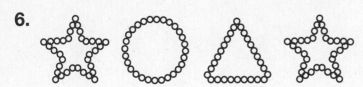

Look at both rows. Draw the next set of beads in each row.

7.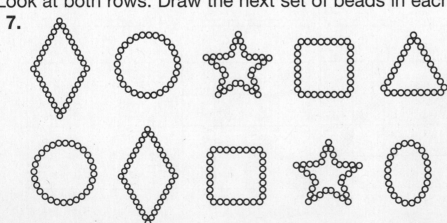

Name _____

Decision Making

You can make warm fleece scarves to sell!

Here's how:

1. 2 feet of fleece fabric makes 3 scarves.

2. Cut the fabric into 3 strips. Each strip will be 6 inches wide.

3. To make a fringe, cut notches on each end. Tie knots in some of the pieces of fringe.

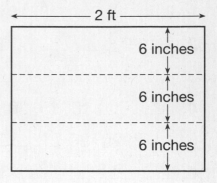

You can buy 2 feet of fabric for $6. You can sell each scarf for any price you wish.

1. a. How many scarves can you make with 2 feet of fabric?

_____

b. How much does 2 feet of fabric cost? _____

c. Suppose you sell 1 scarf for $5. How much will you get for 3 scarves? 3 × $5 = _____

d. How much money will you make from 3 scarves?

_____ − $6 = _____

2. a. How many scarves will you make? _____

b. How much fabric will you buy? _____

c. What will be the price of each scarf? _____

d. How much money will you make? $_____

Patterns in Numbers

Complete the pattern.

1. 2, 4, _____, 8, 10, _____, 14

2. 3, 6, 9, _____, _____, 18

3. 1, 5, 9, _____, _____, _____

4. _____, 10, 15, 20, _____, 30

5. 4, 12, 20, 28, _____, _____

6. _____, _____, 30, 40, 50, 60

7. 4, _____, 12, 16, 20, _____

Make up your own number patterns. Leave two blank spaces. Give them to a classmate to solve.

8. _____, _____, _____, _____, _____, _____

9. _____, _____, _____, _____, _____, _____

10. _____, _____, _____, _____, _____, _____

11. On Sunday night Sylvie had 10 pennies in a jar. If she put 2 more pennies in each morning, how many pennies would she have on Friday night? Skip count on a calendar to find the answer.

_____

12. When do you use number patterns? Think about number patterns in math or other subjects. Think about number patterns at home. Give as many examples as you can.

_____

_____

_____

Visual Thinking

Ring the figures in each row that are the same.

1.

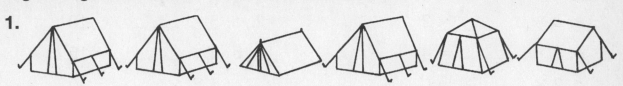

2.

3.

4.

5.

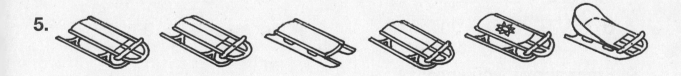

6.

Patterns in Algebra

Complete.

1. a. $2 \times$ _____ $= 2$

   b. $2 \times$ _____ $= 4$

   c. $2 \times$ _____ $= 6$

   d. $2 \times$ _____ $= 8$

2. a. $5 \times$ _____ $= 10$

   b. $5 \times$ _____ $= 15$

   c. $5 \times$ _____ $= 20$

   d. $5 \times$ _____ $= 25$

3. a. $5 \times$ _____ $= 20$

   b. $5 \times$ _____ $= 25$

   c. $5 \times$ _____ $= 30$

   d. $5 \times$ _____ $= 35$

4. a. $2 \times$ _____ $= 12$

   b. $2 \times$ _____ $= 14$

   c. $2 \times$ _____ $= 16$

   d. $2 \times$ _____ $= 18$

5. a. $5 \times$ _____ $= 40$

   b. $5 \times$ _____ $= 45$

   c. $5 \times$ _____ $= 50$

   d. $5 \times$ _____ $= 55$

6. a. $2 \times$ _____ $= 18$

   b. $2 \times$ _____ $= 20$

   c. $2 \times$ _____ $= 22$

   d. $2 \times$ _____ $= 24$

7. a. $5 \times$ _____ $= 15$

   b. _____ $\times 4 = 20$

   c. $5 \times 5 =$ _____

   d. _____ $\times 6 = 30$

8. a. $5 \times$ _____ $= 30$

   b. _____ $\times 7 = 35$

   c. $5 \times 8 =$ _____

   d. _____ $\times 9 = 45$

9. From above, you know

    $5 \times 8 = 40$ and

    $5 \times 9 = 45$.

   How could you find

    5×17?

_____

10. How could you find the product of 2×19?

_____

Critical Thinking

Answer these questions. Use the pictures for help.

1. An adventurer needs to get across the ravine.
   However, the old wooden bridge will break
   if she takes more than 3 steps. Which boards
   should she step on in order to make it? _____

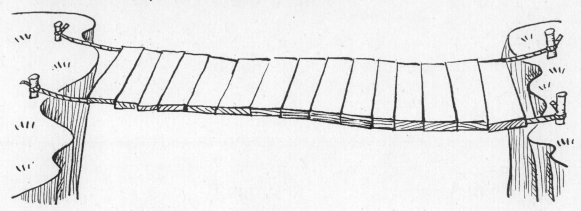

2. If you cross off all the multiples
   of 7 on this chart, you will make
   a diagonal line. What number's
   multiples make 2 diagonal lines
   on this chart?

   _____

1	2	3	4	5	6
X	8	9	10	11	12
13	X4	15	16	17	18
19	20	2X	22	23	24
25	26	27	2X	29	30
31	32	33	34	3X	36

3. What multiples do each of these shaded patterns represent?

   a. Multiples of _____

   b. Multiples of _____

   c. Multiples of _____

   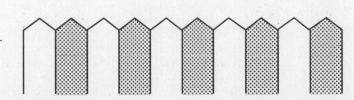

Critical Thinking

Look at the two groups shown for each problem. If you add all the products in each group, which group represents the greater number? Use number sense to figure it out.

1.

Group A	Group B
1×0	0×150
15×1	1×1

a. Which group represents the greater number? _____

b. How do you know?

_____

2.

Group A	Group B
1×21	0×312
122×0	21×0
312×1	1×122

a. Which group represents the greater number? _____

b. How do you know?

_____

3.

Group A	Group B
$1{,}450{,}375 \times 0$	$1{,}450{,}375 \times 1$

a. Which group represents the greater number? _____

b. How do you know?

_____

4. Write your own group question. Use the factors 0 and 1.

_____

_____

Name _____

Patterns in Numbers

Write the next three numbers to continue the pattern. Then
write the rule used to make the pattern.

1. 6, 8, 10, _____, _____, _____

Rule: _____

2. 25, 30, 35, _____, _____, _____

Rule: _____

3. 27, 36, 45 _____, _____, _____

Rule: _____

4. 7, 10, 13, 16, 19, _____, _____, _____

Rule: _____

5. 80, 85, 90, 95, _____, _____, _____

Rule: _____

6. 5, 6, 8, 11, 15, _____, _____, _____

Rule: _____

7. 96, 92, 88, 84, _____, _____, _____

Rule: _____

8. 100, 99, 97, 94, 90, _____, _____, _____

Rule: _____

9. 10, 19, 28, 37, 46, _____, _____, _____

Rule: _____

10. 72, 63, 54, 45, _____, _____, _____

Rule: _____

11. 18, 36, 54, 72, _____, _____, _____

Rule: _____

Critical Thinking

The Mississippi River is often called the "Mighty Mississippi." However, without the help of the Missouri and Ohio Rivers, the Mississippi wouldn't amount to all that much.

The Mississippi is an average-sized river that flows out of Lake Itasca in Minnesota. But it gets bigger near St. Louis, where the Missouri joins it after a 2,466-mile journey. Then the Ohio links up at Cairo, Illinois, after its journey of 980 miles.

By the time the Mississippi finishes its own journey and empties into the Gulf of Mexico, it's one of the longest and most powerful rivers in the world.

1. What kind of information do you know from this article?

_____

_____

2. What information would you like to know that isn't given in the article?

_____

3. Can you find the difference in length between the Mississippi and Missouri rivers? If so, write a number sentence here that shows it.

_____

4. Can you find the difference in length between the Missouri and Ohio rivers? If so, write a number sentence here that shows it.

_____

5. Would you say that the Mississippi is longer or shorter than the Missouri river? What makes you think so?

_____

_____

Critical Thinking

Decide which operation will help you solve each problem.
Then explain how you would solve the problem.

1. You are making invitations for a big family dinner party.
Before you send them, your mother decides to invite
more people. You need to figure out how many
invitations to make.

_____

2. You are baking a cake for the party. The recipe makes
enough batter for a one-layer cake. You would like to
make a two-layer cake. You need to know how much
more of each ingredient to use.

_____

3. You are making snacks for the party. Your father
suggests that you make at least 5 snacks for each
guest. You need to know how many snacks to make.

_____

4. Your family is serving chicken pot-pies at the party. Each
guest gets his or her own pie. At the last minute, some
guests call to say they won't be coming. You need to
know how many pot-pies to bake.

_____

_____

5. You are setting the table for the dinner party. Every place
setting will have two drinking glasses. You need to know
how many drinking glasses to take from the cupboard.

_____

6. Before you relax and enjoy the party you need to make
the fruit drink. Each guest will drink 2 cups. You need to
know how many cups to make.

_____

Critical Thinking

There are 16 groups of 3 in 48. $\quad 16 \times 3 = \textbf{48}$

There are 24 groups of 3 in 72. $\quad 24 \times 3 = \textbf{72}$

There are 41 groups of 3 in 123. $\quad 41 \times 3 = \textbf{123}$

Add the digits in each product above.

1. What is the sum of $4 + 8$? _____

2. What is the sum of $7 + 2$? _____

3. What is the sum of $1 + 2 + 3$? _____

4. Describe the patterns you see. _____

_____

5. How could you use this information to determine if a
number contains an equal number of groups of three?

_____

_____

Use the pattern to predict whether each number contains an
equal number of groups of three. Explain how you made
your prediction.

6. 45 _____

7. 78 _____

8. 103 _____

9. 162 _____

10. 222 _____

11. 263 _____

12. 147 _____

13. 352 _____

Name _____

Visual Thinking

1. These figures are all woggles. How are woggles alike?

_____

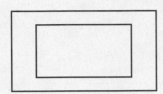 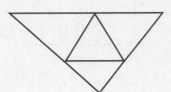

2. Circle the woggle.

   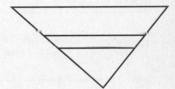

3. These figures are all tripsoms. How are tripsoms alike?

_____

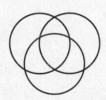 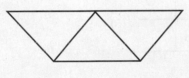 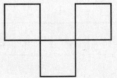 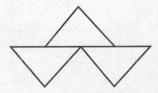

4. Circle the tripsom.

 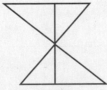

Patterns in Algebra

Complete the table. Write the rule.

1.

In	9	2	5	7	4		8
Out	27	6	15			0	

Rule: _____

2.

In	10	4					7
Out	20	8	16	18	10	2	14

Rule: _____

3.

In	3			9	8	6	4
Out	15	25	35		40		

Rule: _____

4.

In	3	1	7				2
Out	27	9		0	54	36	

Rule: _____

5.

In	9	4	7		8	1	
Out		16		20	32		24

Rule: _____

6.

In	7			3	0	5
Out		12	36			

Rule: _____

Critical Thinking

Mark must read a book for a book report. He has chosen a
book about Mickey Mantle. Mark has made a reading plan.
He will read 7 pages one day, 8 pages the next and continue
this plan.

1. On what day will Mark
start reading Chapter 2?

_____

2. How many pages will Mark
have read after 4 days?

_____

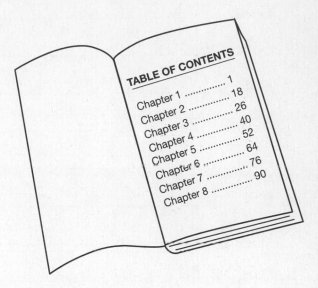

TABLE OF CONTENTS

Chapter 1 1
Chapter 2 18
Chapter 3 26
Chapter 4 40
Chapter 5 52
Chapter 6 64
Chapter 7 76
Chapter 8 90

3. What chapter will Mark be on
after reading for 8 days? How
do you know?

_____

_____

4. On what day will Mark start reading Chapter 8? How do
you know? Explain.

_____

_____

_____

5. The book has 120 pages. Describe how you can find out
how long it will take Mark to finish the book. How many
days will Mark need to finish the book?

_____

_____

Patterns in Numbers

Tell what rule was used to make the pattern. What are the next three numbers?

1. 2, 4, 6, 8, _____, _____, _____

Rule: _____

2. 5, 10, 15, 20, _____, _____, _____

Rule: _____

3. 3, 6, 9, 12, _____, _____, _____

Rule: _____

4. 6, 12, 18, 24, _____, _____, _____

Rule: _____

5. 4, 8, 12, 16, _____, _____, _____

Rule: _____

6. 7, 14, 21, 28, _____, _____, _____

Rule: _____

7. What patterns do you find in **1–6**? Explain.

_____

_____

8. In the pattern that begins 8, 16, 24 . . . what would the 6th number be? _____

9. In the pattern that begins 9, 18, 27 . . . what would the 5th number be? _____

Patterns in Numbers

1	2	3	4	5	6	7	8	9	10
11	12	13	14	15	16	17	18	19	20
21	22	23	24	25	26	27	28	29	30
31	32	33	34	35	36	37	38	39	40
41	42	43	44	45	46	47	48	49	50
51	52	53	54	55	56	57	58	59	60
61	62	63	64	65	66	67	68	69	70
71	72	73	74	75	76	77	78	79	80
81	82	83	84	85	86	87	88	89	90
91	92	93	94	95	96	97	98	99	100

Fill in the blanks with the correct numbers. Use the hundred chart above to help you find the patterns.

1. 3, 6, _____, 12, _____, _____

2. 6, _____, 18, _____, 30, _____

3. _____, 27, 30, _____, _____, 39

4. 36, _____, _____, 54, _____, 66

5. _____, 54, 57, _____, 63, _____

6. 66, 72, _____, _____, _____, 96

7. _____, 39, _____, 45, _____, 51

8. 21, _____, 15, 12, _____, _____

9. 42, 36, _____, _____, 18, _____

10. _____, 93, _____, _____, 84, 81

Patterns in Multiplication

×	0	1	2	3	4	5	6	7	8	9	10	11	12
0	0	0	0	0	0	0	0	0	0	0	0	0	0
1	0	1	2	3	4	5	6	7	8	9	10	11	12
2	0	2	4	6	8	10	12	14	16	18	20	22	24
3	0	3	6	9	12	15	18	21	24	27	30	33	36
4	0	4	8	12	16	20	24	28	32	36	40	44	48
5	0	5	10	15	20	25	30	35	40	45	50	55	60
6	0	6	12	18	24	30	36	42	48	54	60	66	72
7	0	7	14	21	28	35	42	49	56	63	70	77	84
8	0	8	16	24	32	40	48	56	64	72	80	88	96
9	0	9	18	27	36	45	54	63	72	81	90	99	108
10	0	10	20	30	40	50	60	70	80	90	100	110	120
11	0	11	22	33	44	55	66	77	88	99	110	121	132
12	0	12	24	36	48	60	72	84	96	108	120	132	144

Continue each pattern. Use the fact table to help.

1. 7, 14, 21, _____, _____, _____

2. 16, 24, 32, _____, _____, _____

3. 48, 42, 36, _____, _____, _____

4. 27, 36, 45, _____, _____, _____

5. 80, 90, 100, _____, _____, _____

6. 144, 132, 120, _____, _____, _____

7. 121, 100, 81, _____, _____, _____

8. 90, 81, 72, _____, _____, _____

9. 2, 6, 12, _____, _____, _____

10. 0, 1, 4, 9, _____, _____, _____

11. 36, 44, 50, 54, _____, _____, _____

12. 9, 18, 27, _____, _____, 54, _____, 70

Critical Thinking

Your family is going away for 5 days. You are leaving early on Saturday morning. Your neighbor, Mr. Pitt, has agreed to come in at noon each day to feed your two cats while you are away. Each cat needs 3 scoops of dry food each day.

1. How many scoops of food will the cats have been fed after 3 days?

   a. Write the number sentence that will help you solve the problem.

   _____

   b. What is the answer? _____

2. How many scoops of food will Mr. Pitt have fed the cats by the end of the day on Wednesday?

   a. Write the number sentence that will help you solve the problem.

   _____

   b. What is the answer? _____

3. Suppose you also have 3 dogs that eat 5 scoops of dry food each daily. Describe how you can find out how many scoops of food your pets will be fed while you are away.

   _____

   _____

   _____

4. Your friend Alan's family is also going away for 5 days. They have 2 dogs who each eat 4 scoops of food every day. How many scoops will the dogs need to be fed while Alan's family is away?

   _____

Decision Making

You are planning a lunch party. There will be 35 people. Three different restaurants can serve the guests at your party. You need to decide which restaurant to hire.

A. Manny's Restaurant

> **Menu**
> 3 dozen chicken sandwiches
> 8 six-packs of lemonade
> 40 oranges
> Total cost: $210

B. Jill's Cafe

> **Menu**
> 40 ham and cheese sandwiches
> 7 six-packs of juice
> 35 bags of peanuts
> Total cost: $234

C. Doug's Diner

> **Menu**
> 38 turkey sandwiches
> 42 cans of lemonade
> 3 dozen apples
> Total cost: $228

1. Order the choices from most expensive to least expensive.

   _____

   _____

   _____

2. Order the choices from greatest number of food items to least number of food items.

   _____

   _____

   _____

3. If each guest only has one sandwich, one bag of peanuts or piece of fruit, and one drink, how many leftovers will there be for each restaurant choice?

   A. _____

   B. _____

   C. _____

4. Which restaurant would you hire? Why?

   _____

   _____

   _____

Visual Thinking

1. Draw six pieces of pepperoni on the pizza so that each slice gets the same number of pieces of pepperoni.

How many are on each slice? _____

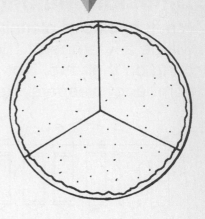

2. Draw twelve pieces of pepperoni on the pizza so that each slice gets the same number of pieces of pepperoni.

How many are on each slice? _____

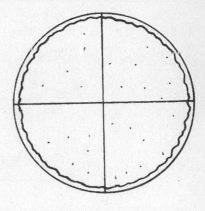

3. Draw twelve pieces of pepperoni on the pizza so that each slice gets the same number of pieces of pepperoni.

How many are on each slice? _____

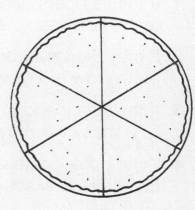

4. Draw fifteen pieces of pepperoni on the pizza so that each slice gets the same number of pieces of pepperoni.

How many are on each slice? _____

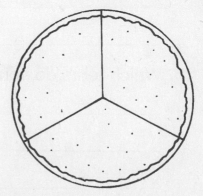

Decision Making

A nature club is planning an overnight camping trip. There will be 24 campers. They need to decide how many tents to bring on their trip. Not all of the tents will shelter the same number of sleepers. Here is a list of the different tent sizes.

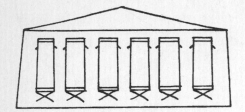

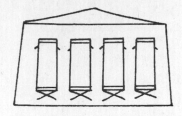

This is the large tent.
It will sleep 6 people.

This is the medium tent.
It will sleep 4 people.

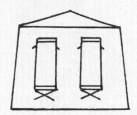

This is the small tent.
It will sleep 2 people.

1. If the campers decide to bring only large tents, how many tents will they need to bring? _____

2. If they decide to bring only medium tents, how many will they need to bring? _____

3. If they decide to bring only small tents, how many will they need to bring? _____

4. What other combinations of tents could they bring so that there is exactly enough room for everyone to sleep?

_____

_____

5. Which tents do you think the club should take? Explain your reasoning.

_____

_____

_____

Critical Thinking

Lisa and 7 of her friends went apple picking. They picked several different kinds of apples. After they were finished picking, they put all of their apples together and counted what they had. They had 24 Macintosh apples, 48 Red Delicious apples, 16 Empire apples, and 8 Cortland apples. They decided that they should share all of the apples equally. Below are 8 bags, one for each person. Decide how many of each kind of apple each person should get, then draw the apples in the bags. Use the letters "M" for Macintosh, "R" for Red Delicious, "E" for Empire, and "C" for Cortland.

How did you decide how many of each type of apple to put in each bag?

_____

_____

Patterns in Numbers

Write the next number in each pattern. Use your knowledge
of multiplication facts.

1. 15, 18, 21, 24, _____

2. 6, 12, 18, 24, _____

3. 21, 28, 35, 42, _____

4. 45, 40, 35, 30, _____

5. 48, 40, 32, 24, _____

Fill in the missing number using your knowledge of
multiplication facts.

6. 16, 20, 24, _____, 32

7. 8, 10, _____, 14, 16

8. 9, _____, 15, 18, 21

9. 49, 42, 35, _____, 21

10. _____, 40, 32, 24, 16

Divide by 2. Then divide the result by 2. Keep dividing by 2
until you cannot go any further.

11. 16

_____

Divide by 3. Then divide the result by 3. Keep dividing by 3
until you cannot go any further.

12. 27

_____

Divide by 4. Then divide the result by 4. Keep dividing by 4
until you cannot go any further.

11. 64

_____

Critical Thinking

1. For each group of eight dots, draw a straight line that divides the dots into two equal groups. Show four different ways to draw the line.

   ● ● ● ●   ● ● ● ●   ● ● ● ●   ● ● ● ●
   ● ● ● ●   ● ● ● ●   ● ● ● ●   ● ● ● ●

2. Find three ways to cut the cake in half so that each half has three cherries on top.

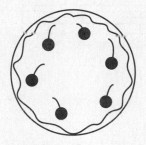 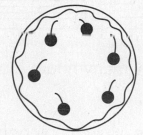 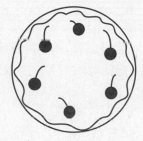

3. Jacob found 28 fossils on his hike. He gave half to his friend. How many did his friend get? _____

4. Mary found 22 rocks on her vacation. She gave half to her sister. How many did Mary keep? _____

5. On Monday, Clara and Beth's grandmother gave them 24 pennies to share equally. How much did each person get?

   _____

6. On Tuesday, Clara and Beth's grandmother gave them 30 pennies to share. How much did each person get?

   _____

7. What strategy did you use to solve **3–6**?

   _____

8. How could you use place value to solve each problem?

   _____

   _____

Critical Thinking

Joe's Market employs 5 workers and pays them each $5 per hour.

1. John makes $30 one day. How many hours did he

work? _____

2. Amy makes $45 over two days. How many hours did

she work? _____

3. Louis earned $35 on Tuesday and $25 on Thursday.
How many hours did he work all together?

_____

4. If John worked for 5 hours, how much money did he

make? _____

5. Omar worked for 8 hours and Jenny worked for 6 hours.

a. How many more hours did Omar work than Jenny? _____

b. How much more money did Omar make than Jenny? _____

6. Louis made $15 on Monday, $20 on Tuesday, and $40 on Wednesday.

a. How many hours did he work on each day?

_____

b. How much did he earn over the three days? _____

c. How much would he have earned if he had
worked twice as long on Monday and half
as long on Wednesday? _____

Name _____

Patterns in Numbers

Fill in the blanks to complete the patterns.

1. 3, 6, 9, _____, _____, _____

2. 12, 16, 20, _____, _____, _____

3. 20, 25, 30, _____, _____, _____

4. 27, 24, 21, _____, _____, _____

5. 35, 30, 25, _____, _____, _____

6. 36, 32, 28, _____, _____, _____

7. 4, 8, _____, 16, _____, _____

8. 6, _____, _____, 15, 18, _____

9. 5, _____, 15, _____, _____, 30

10. 28, 24, _____, _____, 12, _____

11. 21, _____, 15, 12, _____, _____

12. 45, _____, _____, 30, 25, _____

13. 10, _____, 20, _____, 30, _____

14. 32, _____, 24, _____, _____, 12

15. A teacher divides 32 friendship bracelets among 8 students.

   a. How many does each student get? _____

   b. If the students all wear an equal number of friendship bracelets on each wrist, how many does each wear on each wrist? _____

16. Shannon has 18 fruit bars. She gives an equal number to each of 3 friends.

   a. How many fruit bars does each student get? _____

   b. If each friend eats 2 fruit bars a day, how many days will the fruit bars last? _____

Name _____

Visual Thinking

The counters at the left are to be placed in the empty boxes so that there are an equal number of counters in each box. Circle the answer that shows how many counters go in each box. Follow the example.

Example:

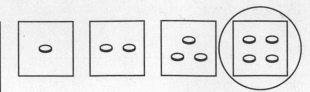

1.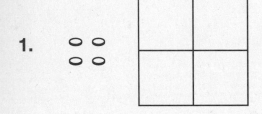

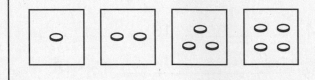

2.

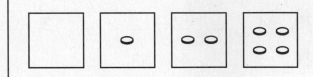

3.

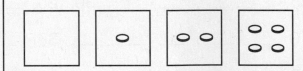

4.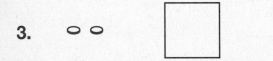

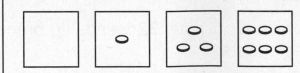

5.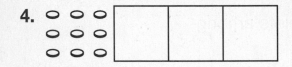

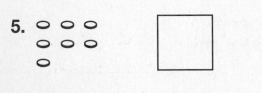

6.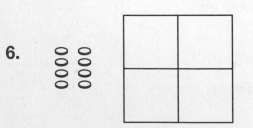

Decision Making

Samantha is looking for an after-school job. She has 3 job offers and must decide which job to take.

A. **Moon Market** A large supermarket. She will bag groceries and stock shelves. She will make $5 for each hour that she works. The store is a 15-minute walk from her house.

B. **Pat's Pet Supply Store** A small pet store. She will sell pet toys and supplies. She will make $3 per hour. The store is a 20-minute bus ride from her house.

C. **Uncle Paul's Corner Store** A very small grocery store. Samantha will work the cash register and bag groceries and stock shelves. She will make $4 per hour. The store is a 2-minute walk from her house.

1. If Samantha works 8 hours each week, how much will she earn at each job?

Job A: _____   Job B: _____   Job C: _____

2. Which job would be the most difficult for traveling from Samantha's house? Explain.

_____

_____

3. Which job do you think would be the most fun? Explain.

_____

_____

4. Which job offer should Samantha take? Explain your reasoning.

_____

_____

_____

Name _____

Patterns in Numbers

Write the next three numbers.
Give the rule for each pattern.

1. 12, 18, 24, 30, _____, _____, _____

Rule: _____

2. 70, 63, 56, 49, _____, _____, _____

Rule: _____

3. 4, 11, 18, 25, _____, _____, _____

Rule: _____

4. 47, 41, 35, 29, _____, _____, _____

Rule: _____

5. 24, 21, 18, 15, _____, _____, _____

Rule: _____

6. 1; 4; 16; 64; _____; _____; _____

Rule: _____

7. 96, 48, 24, _____, _____, _____

Rule: _____

8. 3; 33; 333; _____; _____; _____

Rule: _____

9. 4, 11, 25, 46, _____, _____, _____

Rule: _____

10. Make up your own patterns. Give each rule.

_____

Rule: _____

_____

Rule: _____

Critical Thinking

1. Draw lines to divide each set of squares in half.

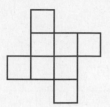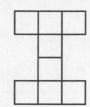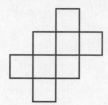

   a. What is 8 ÷ 2? _____

   b. What is 8 ÷ 4? _____

   c. Count the total number of squares.

   What is 24 ÷ 8? _____

2. Draw lines to divide the squares into groups of 9.

   a. How many squares are
   there in all? _____

   b. What is the number of
   squares divided by 9? _____

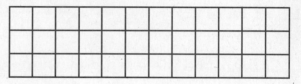

3. 45 flowers are divided among 9 people. How many
   flowers does each person get? _____

4. The Happy Snack Company is giving away free samples
   of dried apricots. It gives away 72 apricots to the first
   9 people.

   a. How many apricots does each person get? _____

   b. The company gives away 56 apricots to the next 8
       people. How many apricots does each person get? _____

5. I have $54. I buy 9 equally priced gifts. How much does
   each one cost? _____

Critical Thinking

Here are two 50 square grids. The first lists the even
numbers from 2 to 50. The second lists the odd numbers
from 1 to 49. Some numbers are missing.

Fill in the missing numbers.

EVEN						ODD				
2	4	6	8	10		1	3	5	7	9
12	14					11				
			28	30					27	
32										39
		46	48	50		41	43			49

1. What patterns can you see in the charts?

_____

_____

2. What are the even numbers between 0 and 50 that end in 6?

_____

3. What are the odd numbers from 0 to 50 that end in 9?

_____

4. a. List the odd multiples of 5 less than 50. _____

    b. List the even multiples of 5 less than 50. _____

    c. Why are some multiples of 5 odd and some even? Explain.

_____

5. Are the multiples of 6 even or odd? _____

6. Are the multiples of 3 even or odd? _____

7. Which numbers, even or odd, have odd multiples? _____

8. Add 4 of the odd numbers. Is your answer an
even or odd number? _____

Decision Making

The reading club at school is having a pizza party. They can afford two large pizzas with 2 toppings but they cannot decide on the toppings. Charles wants to draw a picture and Linda wants to make a list to display all the choices so the club can make a decision. They try both ways.

These toppings are available: sausage, black olives, ham, onions, and green pepper.

Charles' picture

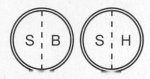

Linda's list

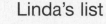

Sausage	Black Olives	Ham	Onions	Green Peppers
✓	✓			
✓		✓		
✓				
✓				

Complete the picture by drawing more pizzas and filling in missing letters. Use S for sausage, B for black olives, H for ham, O for onions and G for green pepper.

Complete the list using check marks.

1. How many different pizzas can they order? _____

2. Which strategy do you think works best in helping the club members decide on which pizzas to order? Explain.

_____

3. Which plan do you think is easier to complete? Why?

_____

_____

4. Which pizza toppings would you choose? _____

Visual Thinking

Draw the shape or shapes that balance each scale.

1. 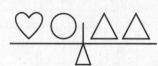 and 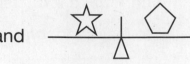 so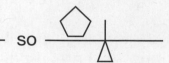

2. 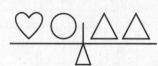 so

3. 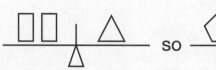 and 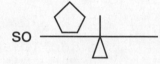 so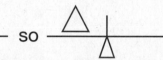

4. 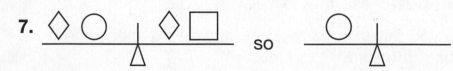 and 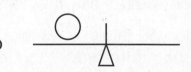 so

5. and 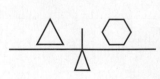 so

6. and so

7. so

8. and so

Visual Thinking

Name the solid figure which answers each riddle. Draw the
figure in the space below each question.

1. I have 1 corner.
I can roll.
What am I?

_____

2. I cannot roll.
I have triangular faces.
What am I?

_____

3. I have 0 flat faces.
I have 0 corners.
What am I?

_____

4. I have 2 flat faces.
I can roll.
What am I?

_____

Name the two solid figures that can be found on each
object.

5.

_____

_____

6.

_____

_____

7.

_____

_____

Visual Thinking

What comes next in the pattern? Draw the shape.

1.

2.

What comes next in the pattern? Draw the solid.

3.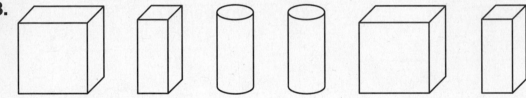

4.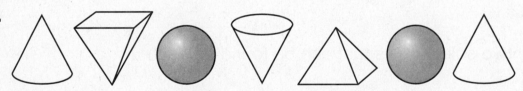

5. Make a new pattern. Use ▢ △ ▢ △ .

Critical Thinking

Look at the drawing. Use it to answer the questions.

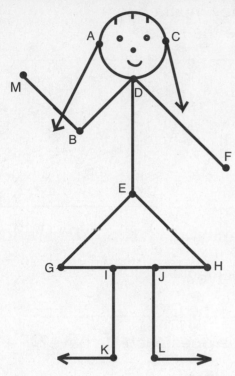

1. How many rays are there? _____

2. What letters label the endpoints of all the rays? _____

3. How many line segments are there? _____

4. Is there a pair of parallel line segments? _____

5. How many lines are there? _____

6. How many endpoints are there? _____

7. Does a line segment intersect a ray? _____

8. Which endpoints have both rays and line segments? _____

9. Between endpoints *G* and *J* and *G* and *H* are

_____

10. Add endpoints to the drawing to create new line segments.

Decision Making

The art club is making a decorative table top. They will paste tiles on a rectangular wooden table top. They must choose one of these three types of tiles to decorate the table.

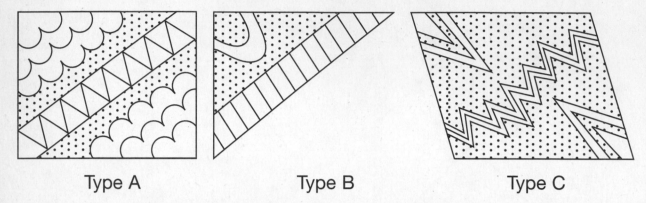

Type A   Type B   Type C

1. How many right angles does each tile have?

   Type A _____   Type B _____   Type C _____

2. How many angles less than a right angle does each tile have?

   Type A _____   Type B _____   Type C _____

3. How many angles greater than a right angle does each tile have?

   Type A _____   Type B _____   Type C _____

4. Which of the tiles would not fit in the corner of the rectangular table top? Why not?

   _____

   _____

5. Think about the work needed to fit each type of tile onto the table top. Which tile would you choose for decorating the table? Why?

   _____

   _____

6. If you wanted to use a greater number of tiles, which would you choose? Why?

   _____

Patterns in Geometry

Find the pattern in each row by identifying each flip, slide, or turn. Circle the move that comes next.

1.

flip

slide

turn

_____   _____   _____   _____

2.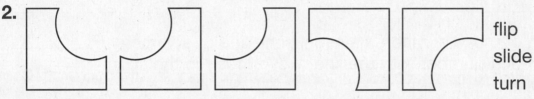

flip

slide

turn

_____   _____   _____

Write whether each figure in the row is congruent or not congruent to the first figure in the row.

3.

_____   _____   _____

_____

4.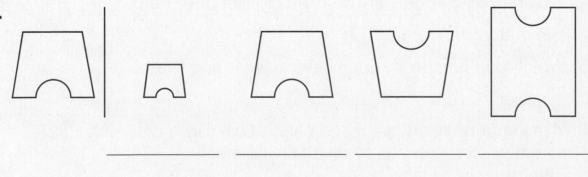

_____   _____   _____

_____   _____   _____

Critical Thinking

1. Write the numbers 0 through 9.

Which of these numbers have no lines of symmetry?
Explain.

_____

_____

2. Which of these numbers have only one line of symmetry? _____
Draw each number with the line of symmetry in the space
below.

3. Which of these numbers have more than one line of symmetry? _____
Draw each number with the lines of symmetry in the space
below.

4. Which even numbers above have at least one line of

symmetry? _____

5. Which odd numbers above have at least one line of

symmetry? _____

6. Write your name in the space below. Draw lines of
symmetry through any symmetrical letters.

Patterns in Geometry

1. How many triangles are in this picture? _____

2. How many squares? _____

3. What is the number of triangles divided by the number of squares? _____

4. Look carefully at the pattern. If one more square and one more set of triangles were drawn around the picture following the same pattern, how many more triangles would there be? _____

5. What would the total number of triangles be? _____

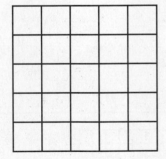

6. How many 1-unit squares are there in this picture? _____

7. How many 4-unit squares are there? _____

8. How many 9-unit squares are there? 16-unit squares? _____

9. What do you notice about all these numbers?

_____

10. How many squares are in this picture in total? _____

Patterns in Geometry

Study the perimeters of these shapes. Ring the shape that doesn't belong in the group.

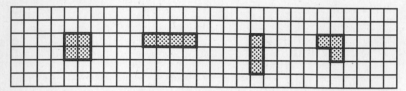

1. Rule: _____

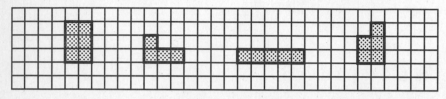

2. Rule: _____

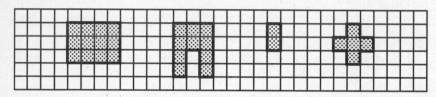

3. Rule: _____

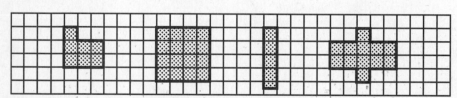

4. Rule: _____

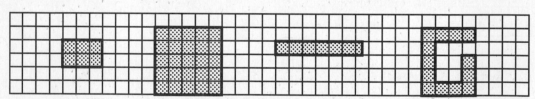

5. Rule: _____

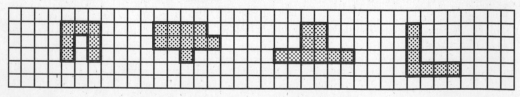

6. Rule: _____

Critical Thinking

1. What are the areas of the five rectangles inside the square grid?

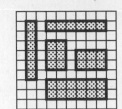

_____

2. What is the area of the large square grid?

_____

3. If you color each rectangle red, how many unit squares will be red?

Explain how you found you answer. _____

_____

4. If you color the rest of the grid blue, how many unit squares will be blue? Explain your answer.

_____

5. What plan would help find the area of this shape without counting each unit square?

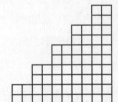

_____

6. Draw lines to divide the shape. How many smaller rectangles do you have?

_____

7. What are the areas of the rectangles?

_____

8. Explain how you found the areas of the rectangles.

_____

9. What is the total area of the shape? Explain how you found the answer.

_____

_____

Name _____

Decision Making

The Science Club is having their winter pizza party. They are going to order thick-crust pan pizza for the dozen members. The pizza comes in three sizes, all rectangular.

A small pizza is 5 inches by 10 inches and costs $4.00.

A medium pizza is 6 inches by 12 inches and costs $6.00.

A large pizza is 10 inches by 15 inches and costs $11.00.

1. Draw arrays on grid paper to show the three sizes of pizza.

   Have one square on the grid paper equal one inch.

   Find the area of each size of pizza.

   Small _____ Medium _____

   Large _____

2. The last time the club ordered pizza they ordered one large pizza but they didn't have enough. Some members say they should order two large pizzas this time. Some members suggest they order small or medium pizzas and save money.

   What should the club members consider when placing their order this time?

   _____

   _____

   _____

   _____

3. The club estimates that they could have eaten about 250 square inches of pizza last time. What would you suggest? Explain your decision.

   _____

   _____

   _____

Visual Thinking

A face is one side of a figure. A cube has 6 faces.

Use cubes to build this shape. Then answer each question.

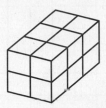

1. On how many cubes can you see
   three faces? _____

2. On how many cubes can you see
   only two faces? _____

3. On how many cubes can you see
   only one face? _____

4. How many cubes are hidden from view? _____

5. What is the volume of this figure in cubic units? _____

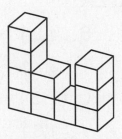

6. What is the volume of this figure in cubic units? _____

7. The volume of this figure was originally 16 cubic
   units before a piece was removed. What is the
   volume of the missing piece? _____

8. Draw the missing piece.

Visual Thinking

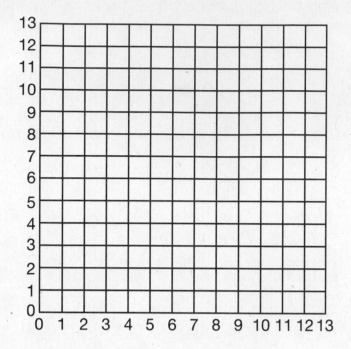

Use the grid. Draw a point at each ordered pair.

The first number shows how many spaces you move to the right. The second number shows how many spaces you move up.

Label each point with the corresponding letter.

Connect the letters in order from A to Z.

A (7,3)	J (13,11)	S (1,8)
B (8,5)	K (12,12)	T (3,7)
C (10,4)	L (11,11)	U (2,5)
D (11,3)	M (9,9)	V (1,3)
E (13,1)	N (7,7)	W (1,1)
F (13,3)	O (5,9)	X (3,3)
G (12,5)	P (3,11)	Y (4,4)
H (11,7)	Q (2,12)	Z (6,5)
I (13,8)	R (1,11)	

What do you see? _____

Color your graph.

Patterns in Numbers

Complete the pattern.

1. 20, 40, _____, 80, 100, _____

2. 40, 80, _____, 160, _____, 240

3. 90, 180, _____, 360, _____, _____

4. 30, 60, 90, _____, _____, 180

5. 70, 140, 210, _____, _____, _____

6. _____, _____, 180, 240, 300, _____

7. _____, 100, 150, 200, _____, _____

8. 80, _____, 240, 320, _____, _____

Make up your own number patterns. Leave two blank spaces
Give them to a classmate to solve.

9. _____, _____, _____, _____, _____, _____

10. _____, _____, _____, _____, _____, _____

11. _____, _____, _____, _____, _____, _____

12. Suppose a number pattern starts with the two numbers
shown. Finish the pattern two different ways.

a. 10, 20, _____, _____, _____

b. 10, 20, _____, _____, _____

Critical Thinking

Look at the product. Then write the number that would be multiplied by 10 to get that product.

1. 210 _____   **2.** 300 _____

3. 240 _____   **4.** 150 _____

5. 180 _____   **6.** 320 _____

7. 80 _____   **8.** 360 _____

9. 750 _____   **10.** 520 _____

Look at the product. Then write the number that would be multiplied by 100 to get that product.

11. 3,000 _____   **12.** 2,400 _____

13. 4,200 _____   **14.** 500 _____

15. 1,500 _____   **16.** 1,800 _____

17. 2,000 _____   **18.** 4,800 _____

19. 7,500 _____   **20.** 6,400 _____

Look at the product. Then write two possible factors for that product.

21. 210 _____   **22.** 3,500 _____

23. 350 _____   **24.** 4,800 _____

25. 150 _____   **26.** 1,800 _____

27. 2,400 _____   **28.** 3,600 _____

29. 1,600 _____   **30.** 3,500 _____

Name _____

Decision Making

The school is building a parking lot 100 feet by 160 feet.

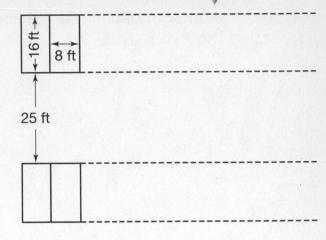

- A parking space is about 16 feet by 8 feet.
- There will be 25 feet between each row.
- 34 teachers, 2 principals, and 3 school secretaries drive to work each day.
- At least 4 parking spaces are needed for visitors

Plan the parking lot.

1. How many parking spaces do you need?

_____

2. How many parking spaces will you put in each row? Explain.

_____

_____

3. How many rows will you have? Explain.

_____

_____

_____

4. Make a decision. What will your parking lot look like? Draw it on a separate sheet of paper.

5. Is there another way to plan the parking lot? Would there be as many spaces?

_____

Visual Thinking

Find the other half of each object below. Draw a line connecting the two halves.

1.

2.

3.

4.

5.

6.

Critical Thinking

Complete each pattern in two different ways. Tell the rule.

1. a. 1, 2, _____, _____, _____

Rule: _____

b. 1, 2, _____, _____, _____

Rule: _____

2. a. 3, 6, _____, _____, _____

Rule: _____

b. 3, 6, _____, _____, _____

Rule: _____

3. a. 10, 30, _____, _____, _____

Rule: _____

b. 10, 30, _____, _____, _____

Rule: _____

4. a. 40, 80, _____, _____, _____

Rule: _____

b. 40, 80, _____, _____, _____

Rule: _____

Critical Thinking

Suppose you are helping the school secretary with the new
book orders. Here is the order list so far:

Title	Boxes Ordered	Books per Box
City Mouse, Country Mouse	8	24
Lyle Goes to the Office	6	36
City Wheels	5	48

1. For which book is the greatest number of copies on order?

   _____

2. Suppose 3 boxes of each book arrive.
   How many more books are still expected?   _____

3. How many more copies of *Lyle Goes to the Office*
   are on order than *City Mouse, Country Mouse*?   _____

4. Mr. Matlaw, the librarian, wants an equal number of
   copies of each book for the after-school reading
   program. What's the least number of boxes he should
   order of each title?

   a. *City Mouse, Country Mouse*:   _____

   b. *Lyle Goes to the Office*:   _____

   c. *City Wheels*:   _____

   d. Describe how you found your answer.

   _____

   _____

5. Mr. Matlaw wants to order 4 boxes of *Wind in the
   Willows*. If there are 12 books in each box, how
   many books will he receive?   _____

Decision Making

Your club is planning a big trip to visit a distant city. You want to know if your club can afford it. There are 7 members. Your club president made a list of travel costs to 4 of your favorite cities.

From Albuquerque to:	One Round-Trip Ticket Costs:
New York City	$450
Chicago	$480
Los Angeles	$270
Miami	$390

1. How much will it cost the club to go to

   a. New York? _____

   b. Chicago? _____

   c. Los Angeles? _____

   d. Miami? _____

2. During the last 2 years, your club has raised $2,500. If you vote to use this money towards your trip, which city do you think would be a good choice? Why?

   _____

   _____

3. If each club member could raise an additional $100, what other cities would be good choices?

   _____

4. Two club members realize they cannot go on the trip. Will the club's $2,500 be enough for the remaining members to go to Chicago? Explain.

   _____

5. What additional costs besides airfare should your club consider?

   _____

Visual Thinking

Look at each set of figures. Think about how the two images
on the left are alike or different. Then, circle the pair of
images on the right that have the same relationship.

1.

2.

3.

4. ¢ : ¢¢

¢ : $ $: ¢

$: $$ ¢ : $$

Patterns in Data

Study the patterns created by the symbols, letters, or numbers. Then, write the next three symbols, letters, or numbers that continue the pattern.

1. ⚐, ∞, ⚐, ∞, ⚐, ∞, ⚐, ∞, ⚐, ∞, _____, _____, _____

2. $, $, ¢, ¢, ¢, $, $, ¢, ¢, ¢, $ _____, _____, _____

3. ^, ^, ^, !, ^, ^, ^, !, ", ", ", _____, _____, _____

4. +, =, +, +, =, +, +, =, +, _____, _____, _____

5. #, #, #, #, ?, #, #, #, ?, #, #, _____, _____, _____

6. <, <, >, >, <, >, <, <, >, >, _____, _____, _____

7. P, L, S, T, S, L, P, L, S, T, S, _____, _____, _____

8. A, A, E, E, I, A, A, E, E, I, A, A, _____, _____, _____

9. A, A, E, I, I, O, U, U, A, E, _____, _____, _____

10. 2, 4, 5, 7, 8, 10, 11, 13, 14, 16, _____, _____, _____

Decision Making

The Craft Fair is coming up! Your class has 7 weeks to make 154 pencil holders.

Some weeks, you work faster than others. The class made 20 pencil holders by the end of the first week, 35 by the end of the 2nd week, 55 by the end of the 3rd week, and 70 by the end of the 4th week. There are 3 weeks left.

1. If you let this pattern continue will you have at least 154 pencil holders in 3 more weeks? Explain.

_____

2. Describe 1 way the class can complete the remaining pencil holders on time.

_____

_____

3. Every other week your class goes to the library and is away from school for a half day. This is why the class didn't make as many pencil holders the 2nd and 4th week. Complete the table. How many pencil holders should the class make each week to meet their goal of 154 pencil holders?

Week	1	2	3	4	5	6	7
Number made during week	20	15	20	15			
Total pencil holders made	20	35	55	70			

4. Your class sells the pencil holders for $2 each. How much money would they have made if they had stopped making pencil holders after 4 weeks? _____

Critical Thinking

The people who live at the River Front Apartments need more parking spaces. They plan to add 14 new rows! They want to assign some of the new rows to each building. Here's what they did.

Building	Spaces Needed	Rows Assigned
Building A	120	4 rows
Building B	60	2 rows
Building C	100	5 rows
Building D	90	3 rows

1. How many cars will Building A need to fit in each row? _____

2. How many cars will Building B need to fit in each row? _____

3. How many cars will Building C need to fit in each row? _____

4. How many cars will Building D need to fit in each row? _____

5. The architect wants all the rows to have the same number of parking spaces. What can she do?

_____

_____

6. How many parking spaces are needed all together?

_____

7. a. Suppose the buildings shared rows. How many rows would they need if each row had 7 parking spaces? _____

   b. Explain how you solved a.

_____

_____

Visual Thinking

Look at the shapes on the left in each row. All of the shapes but one are used to make the picture on the right. Circle the shape on the left that is not used.

1.

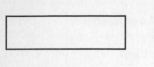   

2.

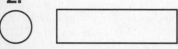   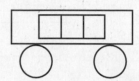

3.

4.

5.

6.

       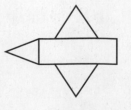

Critical Thinking

You'll need to work backward with quotients and
remainders to solve these problems!

Circle the correct answers.

1. Angela gave 6 of her friends each a stick of gum and
   had 2 left over. How many sticks of gum did she have to
   start with?

   a. 10 sticks   **b.** 6 sticks   **c.** 8 sticks   **d.** 6 sticks

2. Robert used 13 apples to make 3 apple turnovers. He
   had 1 apple left over. How many apples did he use in
   each turnover?

   a. 4 apples   **b.** 3 apples   **c.** 5 apples   **d.** 2 apples

3. San Ho made enough granola to fill 5 tins. Each tin holds
   4 pounds. He has 3 pounds left over. How many pounds
   of granola did San Ho make?

   a. 16 pounds   **b.** 20 pounds   **c.** 14 pounds   **d.** 23 pounds

4. Amir had 48 soup cans to stack on his family's store
   shelves. 9 cans fit on each shelf. He had 3 cans left over.
   How many shelves did Amir stack with soup cans?

   a. 3 shelves   **b.** 5 shelves   **c.** 2 shelves   **d.** 6 shelves

5. The Save-the-Earth Club collected enough trash to fill
   4 bags. Each bag holds 5 gallons. They have 2 gallons
   left over. How much trash did they collect?

   a. 22 gallons   **b.** 36 gallons   **c.** 50 gallons   **d.** 31 gallons

6. Each page of Glen's album holds 4 photographs. He
   filled all 9 pages and still had 3 photos left over. How
   many photos did Glen have to start with?

   a. 35 photos   **b.** 22 photos   **c.** 25 photos   **d.** 39 photos

7. Kelly gave 4 friends each 4 trading cards and kept 3 for
   herself. How many cards did she have to start with?

   a. 16 cards   **b.** 11 cards   **c.** 19 cards   **d.** 24 cards

Patterns in Numbers

What happens to quotients of the same number when divisors change? Solve these problems and look for patterns.

1. a. $31 \div 4 =$ _____

   b. $31 \div 5 =$ _____

   c. $31 \div 6 =$ _____

   d. $31 \div 7 =$ _____

   e. $31 \div 8 =$ _____

   f. $31 \div 9 =$ _____

2. a. $33 \div 3 =$ _____

   b. $33 \div 4 =$ _____

   c. $33 \div 5 =$ _____

   d. $33 \div 6 =$ _____

   e. $33 \div 7 =$ _____

   f. $33 \div 8 =$ _____

3. a. $47 \div 9 =$ _____

   b. $47 \div 8 =$ _____

   c. $47 \div 7 =$ _____

   d. $47 \div 6 =$ _____

   e. $47 \div 5 =$ _____

4. a. $50 \div 9 =$ _____

   b. $50 \div 8 =$ _____

   c. $50 \div 7 =$ _____

   d. $50 \div 6 =$ _____

   e. $50 \div 5 =$ _____

5. Describe the patterns that you see.

_____

_____

_____

Critical Thinking

Your school is having a craft fair in the auditorium. Sellers will rent tables that are 10 feet long. There will be two rows of tables. One row of tables will go against each of the two long walls of the auditorium. These walls are 56 feet long.

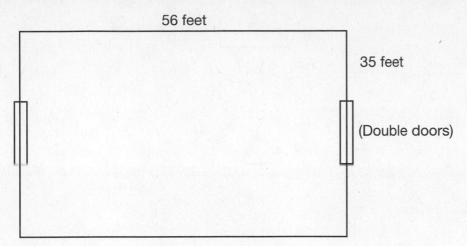

56 feet

35 feet

(Double doors)

Solve each problem. You may use the picture to help you.

1. How many tables can fit in the auditorium all together? Show how you got your answer. Draw the tables in the diagram above.

_____

_____

2. 3 people (a potter, a woodworker, and a painter) each want to rent 2 tables. How many tables are left for other people to rent? Label the tables in the diagram above.

_____

3. If your school wants to raise $500 by renting tables at the fair, how much should people pay per table? Explain you got your answer.

_____

Visual Thinking

Find the part that completes each shape below. Draw a line connecting the two pieces.

1.

2.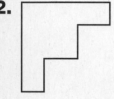

3.

4.

5.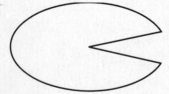

6.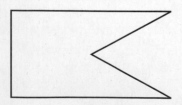

Decision Making

You have been asked to design flags for your school's annual fair. Each grade needs their own flag.

Color the flags according to the instructions.

1. Grade 1 wants $\frac{1}{2}$ of their flag red.

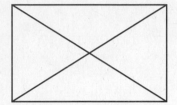

2. Grade 2 wants $\frac{2}{3}$ of their flag green.

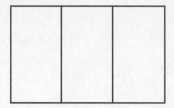

3. Grade 3 wants $\frac{3}{4}$ of the circle orange.

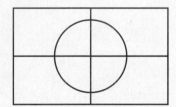

4. Grade 4 wants $\frac{3}{8}$ of their flag blue.

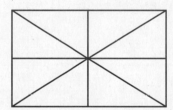

5. Grade 5 wants $\frac{1}{2}$ of their flag red and $\frac{1}{4}$ of the flag blue.

6. Grade 6 wants $\frac{1}{2}$ of the triangles red and $\frac{1}{2}$ of the rest of the flag green.

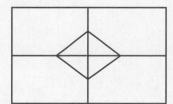

Patterns in Numbers

Tell what rule was used to make the pattern. Complete the next three fractions.

1. $\frac{1}{2}$, $\frac{2}{4}$, $\frac{3}{6}$, $\frac{4}{\boxed{}}$, $\frac{5}{\boxed{}}$, $\frac{6}{\boxed{}}$

Rule: _____

_____

2. $\frac{3}{4}$, $\frac{6}{8}$, $\frac{9}{12}$, $\frac{12}{\boxed{}}$, $\frac{15}{\boxed{}}$, $\frac{18}{\boxed{}}$

Rule: _____

_____

3. $\frac{1}{5}$, $\frac{2}{10}$, $\frac{3}{15}$, $\frac{\boxed{}}{20}$, $\frac{\boxed{}}{25}$, $\frac{\boxed{}}{30}$

Rule: _____

_____

4. $\frac{1}{18}$, $\frac{1}{15}$, $\frac{1}{12}$, $\frac{1}{\boxed{}}$, $\frac{1}{\boxed{}}$, $\frac{1}{\boxed{}}$

Rule: _____

5. $\frac{1}{2}$, $\frac{1}{4}$, $\frac{1}{8}$, $\frac{1}{16}$, $\frac{1}{\boxed{}}$, $\frac{1}{\boxed{}}$ $\frac{1}{\boxed{}}$

Rule: _____

6. $\frac{1}{3}$, $\frac{2}{6}$, $\frac{3}{9}$, $\frac{4}{12}$, $\frac{\boxed{}}{15}$, $\frac{\boxed{}}{18}$, $\frac{\boxed{}}{21}$

Rule: _____

_____

Name _____

Critical Thinking

Some friends want to share a pizza. Read what they say.
Then write the letter of the slice to give each person.

1. "I want $\frac{1}{4}$ of the pizza," said Kate. _____

2. "I want more than Kate," said Miguel. _____

3. "I want half as much as Miguel," said Rosemarie. _____

4. "I want less than Rosemarie," said Joe. _____

5. "I want as much as Joe," said Hollis. _____

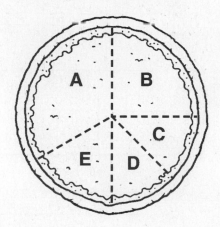

6. Write and illustrate your own pizza problem. Give it to a
   friend to solve.

   _____

   _____

   _____

Name _____

Visual Thinking

Estimate the fractional part shown by the shading in each picture.
Circle the two shapes that show about the same fraction.

1.

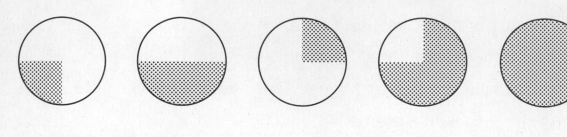

_____ _____ _____ _____ _____

2.

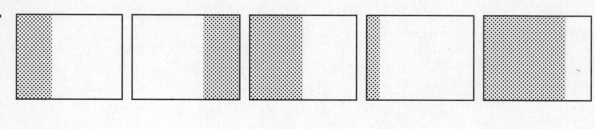

_____ _____ _____ _____ _____

3.

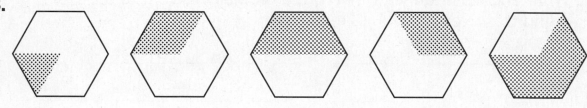

_____ _____ _____ _____ _____

4.

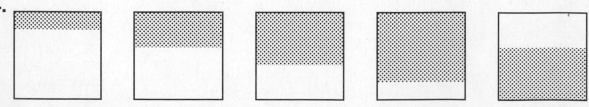

_____ _____ _____ _____ _____

Visual Thinking

This picture shows the number 1:

Compare each picture to the square above. Circle the picture that shows each fractional part.

1. $\frac{1}{2}$

a.　　　b.　　　c.　　　d.

2. $\frac{1}{3}$

a.　　　b.　　　c.　　　d.

3. $\frac{1}{10}$

a.　　　b.　　　c. 　　　d.

4. $\frac{2}{5}$

a.　　　b.　　　c.　　　d.

5. $\frac{3}{4}$

a.　　　b. 　　　c. 　　　d.

Decision Making

For each problem, predict which choice is best. Then solve the problem to test your prediction.

1. There are 36 students in your class and $\frac{1}{3}$ of them are going on a field trip. If you want to bring a snack for everyone, which choice is best?

   A. three 3-packs of giant oatmeal cookies

   B. three 4-packs of granola bars

   C. ten pieces of carrot cake

   a. What is your prediction for the best choice? _____

   b. How many students are going on the trip? _____

   c. Which choice will give you this many servings? _____

2. When you are on vacation, you decide to send postcards to $\frac{1}{4}$ of your class. You have 6 other friends who are not in your class to whom you will send postcards. Postcards are sold in different sized packages. Which choice is best?

   A. two 8-card packs

   B. one 12-card pack

   C. three 4-card packs

   a. What is your prediction for the best choice? _____

   b. How many postcards will you send to students in your class? _____

   c. How many postcards will you send in total? _____

   d. Which choice is best? _____

Critical Thinking

Uncle Stan is a food critic for your local newspaper. He eats at restaurants and judges the food. Use his latest Restaurant Ratings to answer each question.

Stan's Restaurant Guide		
Downtown Cosmic Café	$ $ ¢	☆ ☆
Joe's Grill	$ ¢	☆ ☆ ☆
Daphne's Dinner Emporium	$ $ $	☆
Pierre's House of Crêpes	$ ¢	☆ ☆
The Koffee Klutch	$	☆ ☆ ☆

$ cheap $ $ expensive $ $ $ very expensive
☆ O.K.   ☆ ☆ good   ☆ ☆ ☆ very good

1. Why do some restaurants have half dollar signs or half stars listed after their name?

_____

_____

2. How many dollar signs did Uncle Stan give to the following? Write your answer as a mixed number.

   a. Downtown Cosmic Café   _____

   b. Pierre's House of Crêpes   _____

3. How many stars did Uncle Stan award to the following? Write your answer as a whole or mixed number.

   a. The Koffee Klutch   _____

   b. Joe's Grill   _____

Patterns in Numbers

Write the next three numbers in the pattern. Then describe
the rule.

1. $\frac{1}{2}$, $\frac{2}{3}$, $\frac{3}{4}$, _____, _____, _____

Rule: _____

2. $\frac{1}{4}$, $\frac{2}{4}$, $\frac{3}{4}$, _____, _____, _____

Rule: _____

3. $\frac{1}{6}$, $\frac{2}{12}$, $\frac{3}{18}$, _____, _____, _____

Rule: _____

4. $\frac{2}{3}$, $\frac{6}{9}$, $\frac{18}{27}$, _____, _____, _____

Rule: _____

5. $\frac{3}{5}$, $\frac{6}{15}$, $\frac{12}{45}$, _____, _____, _____

Rule: _____

6. $\frac{32}{64}$, $\frac{16}{32}$, $\frac{8}{16}$, _____, _____, _____

Rule: _____

7. $\frac{729}{16}$, $\frac{243}{16}$, $\frac{81}{16}$, _____, _____, _____

Rule: _____

8. $\frac{1}{2}$, $\frac{1}{2}$, $\frac{2}{2}$, $\frac{3}{2}$, $\frac{5}{2}$, _____, _____, _____

Rule: _____

Decision Making

There is a big party tonight. You will be in charge of serving the food.

Cut the food pictured below into equal servings to give each person the amount they need. Then explain what you did.

1. There are 21 people at the party. Everyone gets at least 1 piece of pizza. Draw lines to show how you would cut the pizzas.

   Explain how you made your decision.

   _____

   _____

   _____

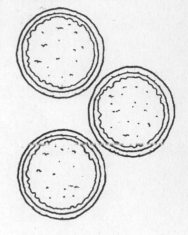

2. There are 18 people at the party. Everyone gets at least 1 piece of corn bread. Draw lines to show how you would cut the bread.

   Explain how you made your decision.

   _____

   _____

   _____

3. There are 10 people at the party. Everyone gets at least 2 pieces of pie. Draw lines to show how you would cut the pies.

   Explain how you made your decision.

   _____

   _____

   _____

Visual Thinking

Circle the figure that is the same length as the first figure.

1.

2.

3.

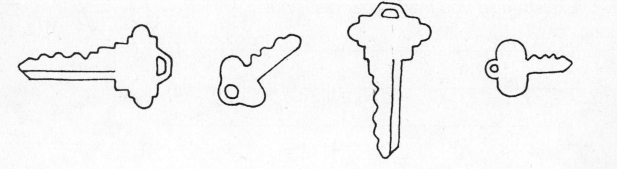

4.

5.

Patterns in Measurement

Use your ruler to measure the length of each item. Write a
rule to describe each pattern. Draw the item that would
come next.

1.

Rule: _____

2.
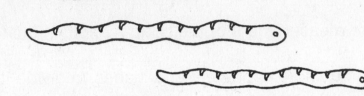

Rule: _____

3.

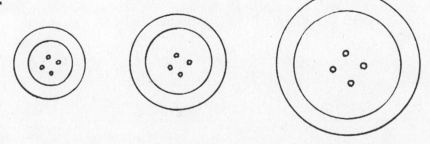

Rule: _____

4.
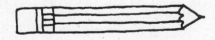

Rule: _____

Name _____

Critical Thinking

The school librarian just received 27 new books. She needs to put them in a bookcase. To figure out how to arrange the books, she estimated the width of each book.

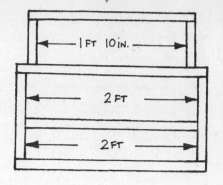

15 books are about 2 inches wide each
8 books are about 3 inches wide each
4 books are about 4 inches wide each

1. What is the measurement of the top shelf, in inches? _____

2. What is the measurement of the second shelf, in inches? _____

3. What is the measurement of the bottom shelf, in inches? _____

4. Use what you know about feet and inches to divide the books into three groups that will fit on the 3 shelves.

a. How many of each type of book should be placed on the top shelf?

_____

b. How many of each type of book should be placed on the second shelf?

_____

_____

c. How many of each type of book should be placed on the bottom shelf?

_____

_____

5. Add the widths of all the books combined. Give your answer in feet and inches.

_____

Visual Thinking

Suppose you fold a piece of paper in half and then punch holes with a hole punch.

In each row, the drawing on the left shows the paper folded in half. Circle the drawing on the right that shows what the paper will look like when it is unfolded.

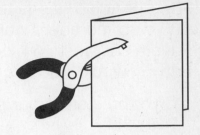

1.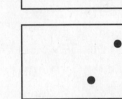

2.

3.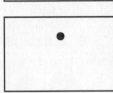

Suppose you fold a sheet of paper in half twice before you punch holes. Circle the figure on the right that shows what the paper will look like when it is unfolded.

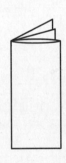

4.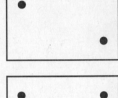

5.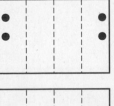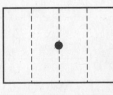

6.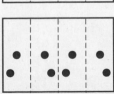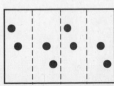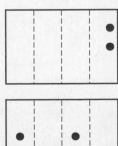

Decision Making

A soccer club needs to raise money for new uniforms. A survey of how 100 club members want to raise the money shows that 57 would like to have a car wash, 64 would sell magazines, 49 would bake for a bake sale, and 71 would ride in a Bike-a-thon.

1. Complete the bar graph to show this data.

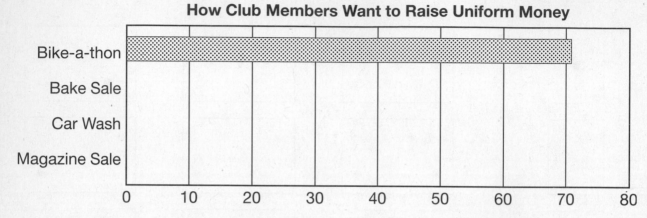

How Club Members Want to Raise Uniform Money

2. Suppose you are the club President. You have to decide how to raise the money. What information will you need to make a good decision?

_____

_____

3. What is the number of votes represented in the graph? _____

4. Is this number greater or less than the number of people surveyed? _____

5. What does this tell you about the club members who responded to the survey?

_____

6. How do you think the club should raise money for uniforms? Give reasons for your answer.

_____

_____

_____

Visual Thinking

Circle the model at the right of the equal sign that shows the
answer. Then write the number sentence.

Example

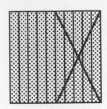 =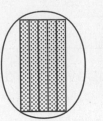

__10__ – __5__ = __5__

1.

_____ + _____ = _____

2.

_____ – _____ = _____

3.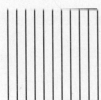

_____ + _____ = _____

4.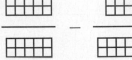

_____ – _____ = _____

Critical Thinking

Twelve students in your gym class run a 50-meter race. Here are their times in seconds:

9.90	9.99	8.51	9.09	9.9	8.49
8.5	9.01	8.98	9.11	9.10	9.95

1. Write the times above in order from greatest to least.

_____

_____

2. Are there any numbers that are equal? _____

   If so, write the equal numbers. _____

3. Zachary finished the race first. What was his running time? _____

4. Tad took the greatest amount of time to finish. What was his time?

   _____

5. Charlie finished in fifth place. What was his time? _____

6. Susie finished in eighth place. What was her time? _____

7. Write the finishing times from fastest to slowest.

_____

8. Is there a difference between your answer to **1** and your answer to **7**? Explain.

_____

_____

9. Suppose the third place finisher runs in another race. This time she finishes 0.10 seconds earlier. What was her time in seconds?

_____

Patterns in Numbers

Write numbers to complete the patterns. Then write the rule you used.

1. 0.1, $\frac{1}{10}$, 0.2, $\frac{2}{10}$, 0.3, $\frac{3}{10}$ _____, _____

Rule: _____

2. 1.2, $1\frac{3}{10}$, 1.4, $1\frac{5}{10}$, 1.6, $1\frac{7}{10}$, _____, _____

Rule: _____

_____

3. $3\frac{1}{10}$, 2.8, $2\frac{5}{10}$, 2.2, $1\frac{9}{10}$, 1.6, _____, _____

Rule: _____

_____

4. four tenths, 0.8, $1\frac{2}{10}$, one and six tenths, 2.0, $2\frac{4}{10}$,

_____, _____, _____

Rule: _____

_____

5. 0.1, $\frac{5}{10}$, 0.9, $1\frac{3}{10}$, _____, _____, _____, _____

Rule: _____

_____

6. $2\frac{4}{10}$, 2.1, $1\frac{8}{10}$, 1.5, _____, _____, _____

Rule: _____

_____

7. 0.9, $1\frac{5}{10}$, 2.1, $2\frac{7}{10}$, 3.3, _____, _____, _____

Rule: _____

_____

Decision Making

You are planning a small party for six people. You will be serving cake and juice. You have $10.00 to spend on party supplies. Here is a list of prices from your local grocery store.

Party Supplies	
12 napkins	$1.13
6 party horns	$2.07
8 large paper plates	$1.77
10 plastic forks	$1.50
1 package of multi-colored streamers	$0.75
6 plastic knives	$1.04
12 plastic spoons	$2.23
Welcome banner	$2.12
8 small paper plates	$0.98
6 party hats	$2.71
8 plastic cups	$1.40
12 multi-colored balloons	$1.39

1. List the supplies that are used for eating and drinking. What is the total cost of these supplies?

   _____

   _____

   _____

   _____

2. List the rest of the supplies in order from most to least expensive. What is the total cost?

   _____

   _____

3. You need to decide which supplies you will buy with $10.00.

   a. Do you have enough money to buy all of the supplies on the list?

   _____

   b. Write the supplies that you would choose to buy.

   _____

   c. Which supplies did you decide not to buy? Why?

   _____

   _____

   _____

   _____

Critical Thinking

Ms. Ortiz's language arts class is performing some scenes from a play. Nick and Anita are in charge of costumes. They need to purchase some fabric, lace, and ribbon. Fabric is sold by the yard; lace and ribbon are sold by the foot.

Here is a list of the items that they would like to purchase:

Item	Cost
5 yards of blue cotton fabric	$1.70 per yard
2 feet of silver sparkle lace	$0.70 per foot
5 feet of white lace ribbon	$0.40 per foot
7 yards of purple felt fabric	$0.70 per yard
2 feet of thin lace	$0.50 per foot
12 feet of satin ribbon	$0.25 per foot
4 yards of white linen fabric	$0.40 per yard

1. How much money will they need to make their purchase?

_____

2. Describe how you found the total cost.

_____

_____

3. Suppose all the fabric cost $1.05 per yard and all the lace and ribbon cost $0.30 per foot. Find the new total cost. _____

4. Describe a second way you could solve **3**.

_____

_____

_____

_____

Critical Thinking

Maria's Number Trick		Matt's Number	Ruth's Number
1.	Pick a number from 0 to 10.	7	9
2.	Add 6.	13	15
3.	Subtract the number you picked.	6	6
4.	Add 11.	17	17
5.	Is your sum 17?	yes	yes

1. Try the trick with 2 more numbers. Write the number you choose and the sum.

   a. Chosen number: _____   **b.** Chosen number: _____

   Final sum: _____   Final sum: _____

2. The number you get in step 3 is always added to 11. What number do you have to get in step 3 to get a final sum of 17?   _____

3. Look at steps 1, 2, and 3. Explain why you will always get the same sum in step 3, no matter what number you choose.

   _____

   _____

4. Create your own number trick. Make it so that the final result is always the same. Write the steps for your trick below.

   _____

   _____

   _____

Try your trick with two or three numbers to make sure it works. Then try it on a friend.

Visual Thinking

Design a map of your neighborhood. Draw it in the space
below. Include buildings, roads, signs, and any rivers or
lakes. Label each item with the unit of measurement you
would use to measure it. Write cm, m, or km.

Your Home

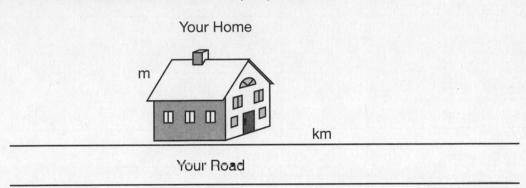

m

km

Your Road

Patterns in Numbers

What are the next four numbers? Tell what rule was used to make the pattern.

1. 44, 42, 40, 38, _____, _____, _____, _____

Rule: _____

2. 3, 6, 12, 24, _____, _____, _____, _____

Rule: _____

3. 1, 4, 9, 16, _____, _____, _____, _____

Rule: _____

4. 13, 20, 27, 34, _____, _____, _____, _____

Rule: _____

5. 4, 20, 100, 500, _____, _____, _____

Rule: _____

6. 74, 71, 68, 65, _____, _____, _____, _____

Rule: _____

7. 2, 4, 8, 16, 32, _____, _____, _____

Rule: _____

8. 729, 243, 81, _____, _____, _____

Rule: _____

9. 4, 15, 26, 37, _____, _____, _____, _____

Rule: _____

10. 2, 5, 11, 23, _____, _____, _____, _____

Rule: _____

Name _____

Extend Your Thinking
12-1

Critical Thinking

Some friends want to share a gallon of juice. Read what they say. Then draw a line to the drinking glass to give each person. Do not draw more than one line to any glass.

1. "I want 2 cups of juice," says Erin.

2. "I want 1 cup less than Erin," says Allison.

3 cups

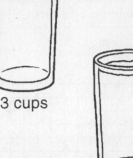
3 cups

3. "I want as much as Erin," says Sean.

4. "I want more than Allison," says Tom.

2 cups

2 cups

5. "I want less than Erin," says Xavier.

6. "I want as much as Tom," says Rosanna.

1 cup

1 cup

7. How many cups of juice are there in all? _____

8. How many pints of juice are left over? _____

9. Who asked for 1 pint of juice? _____

10. Who asked for 1 quart of juice?

_____

Visual Thinking

Circle the two shapes in each row with the same area.

1.

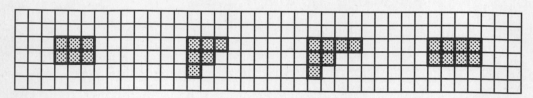

2.

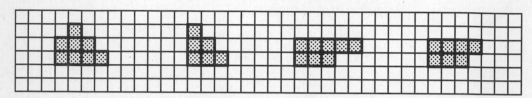

3.

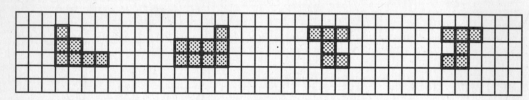

4.

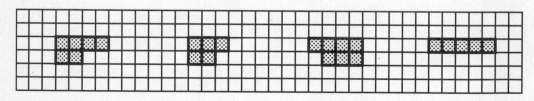

5.

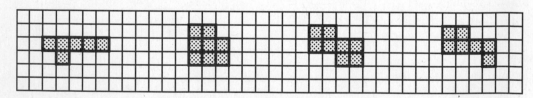

6.

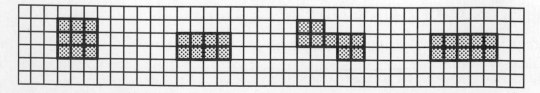

Critical Thinking

Write the correct name under each picture.

1. Max weighs 10 pounds. Kit weighs 3 pounds less than Max. Jake weighs 1 pound more than Kit.

_____ _____ _____

2. Blanco weighs 5 pounds. Fluffy weighs 16 ounces more than Blanco. Bunny weighs 32 ounces less than Fluffy.

_____ _____ _____

3. Daisy weighs the most. Han weighs 16 ounces less than Daisy. Sunny is the lightest.

_____ _____ _____

Decision Making

Ms. McGuire is shipping boxes of oranges. She has $52 to spend on shipping. How many of each size box can she send? She wants to send as many oranges as possible.

4 oranges = 1 kg.

An empty box with 24 spaces for oranges = 1 kg.

An empty box with 36 spaces for oranges = 2 kg.

The shipping company charges Ms. McGuire $2 per kilogram to ship the boxes.

1. How many kilograms is a box filled with
   24 oranges? _____

2. How much will Ms. McGuire spend to ship
   1 box of 24 oranges? _____

3. How many kilograms is a box filled with
   36 oranges? _____

4. How much will Ms. McGuire spend to ship
   1 box of 36 oranges? _____

5. Make a decision. How many of each size box can
   Ms. McGuire send? Explain.

   _____

   _____

   _____

6. Ms. McGuire also wants to send some packets of dried
   apricots. 1 packet is 500 g. (Remember: 500 g is half a kg)

   a. If she has $3 left, how many packets of apricots could
      she send?

      _____

   b. If she needs a box that is 500 g when empty, how
      many packets of apricots could she send?

      _____

Patterns in Numbers

Find the next 3 numbers in each pattern. Then write the rule.

1. 3; 30; 300; _____; _____; _____

Rule: _____

2. 20, 40, 60, _____, _____, _____

Rule: _____

3. 21, 28, 35, _____, _____, _____

Rule: _____

4. 30, 60, 90, _____, _____, _____

Rule: _____

5. 1; 10; 100; _____; _____; _____

Rule: _____

6. 40, 80, 120, _____, _____, _____

Rule: _____

7. 20, 17, 14, 11, _____, _____, _____

Rule: _____

8. 90, 94, 98, _____, _____, _____

Rule: _____

9. 57, 50, 43, _____, _____, _____

Rule: _____

10. 210, 215, 220, _____, _____, _____

Rule: _____

Patterns in Numbers

Write the next three measurements.

1. 1 lb, 16 oz, 2 lb, 32 oz,

_____ , _____ , _____

2. 1 L; 1,000 mL; 3 L; 3,000 mL; 5L;

_____ ; _____ ; _____

3. 2 kg; 4 kg; 6,000 g; 8 kg; 10 kg;

_____ ; _____ ; _____

4. −15°C, −10°C, −5°C, _____ , _____ , _____

5. 72°F, 67°F, 62°F, 57°F, _____ , _____ , _____

6. 8 oz, 1 lb, 24 oz, 2 lb, _____ , _____ , _____

Complete each pattern.

7. 1 cup, 1 pint, _____ , 2 quarts, 1 gallon, _____

8. 20 lb, 17 lb, _____ , 11 lb, _____

9. 70 g, 700 g, _____ , 70 kg, _____

10. 0°C, −3°C, _____ , −9°C, _____

11. 7°F, 14°F, _____ , _____ , 35°F

12. 8 lb, 4 lb, _____ , _____ , _____ 4 oz

13. 1 L, 900 mL, _____ , 700 mL, _____

14. 9 g, 18 g, _____ , _____ , 45 g

Critical Thinking

For each picture, decide if it is possible or impossible.

1. _____

2. _____

3. _____

4. _____

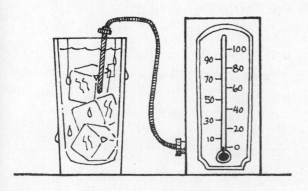

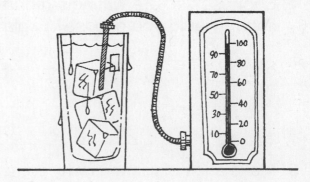

5. _____

6. _____

Decision Making

The city of Carsonville has two libraries.

	Main Library	Branch Library
Books	Three floors full of books Some childrens' books Reference room	Limited selection of books Many childrens' books No encyclopedias
Videos	Limited selection Can check out for 3 days	Hundreds of videos Can check out for 1 day
Story Time	Monday–Friday 4:00–5:00	Every Saturday 12:00–2:00

Other information:

The main library is 1 block from a bus stop.
The branch library is 1 mile from a bus stop.
The main library is 2 blocks from the mall.
The branch library is next to a park.

1. Where would you be more likely to find a particular movie?

_____

2. Where would you be more likely to find a book about spiders?

_____

3. Which library offers more hours of story time?

_____

4. Suppose you are writing a report on Paul Revere. Which library would you choose? Explain your reasoning.

_____

_____

_____

5. Make a list of reasons why someone might choose the branch library.

_____

_____

_____

Patterns in Data

Look at each group of spinners. Tell what rule was used to
make the pattern. Draw the next spinner.

1.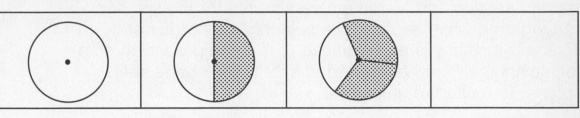

Rule: _____

2.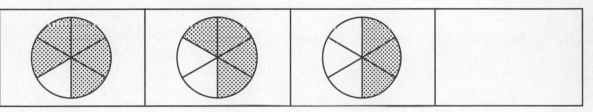

Rule: _____

3.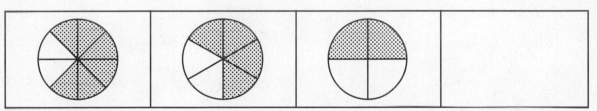

Rule: _____

4.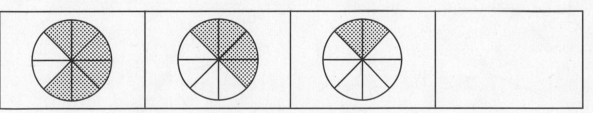

Rule: _____

5. Make up your own pattern using spinners. Leave a blank
in your pattern. Give it to a classmate to complete.

Visual Thinking

Marco and Janine are playing a game using several different spinners. Janine receives points for the spinner landing on a shaded section and Marco receives points for the spinner landing on a white section. The spinners are not fair and Janine is losing! For each question, write the probability that the spinner will land on a shaded spot. Then shade each spinner to make the game fair.

1.
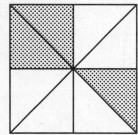

_____

2.
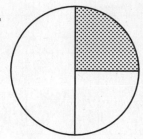

_____

3.
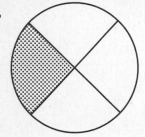

_____

4.
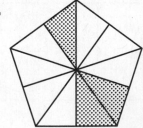

_____

5.
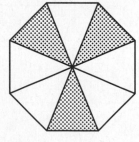

_____

6.
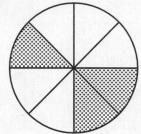

_____

Visual Thinking

Look at each pair of bags. Circle the bag that offers a better chance of choosing a cube.

1.

2.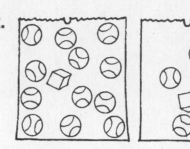

3.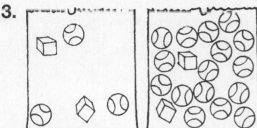

4.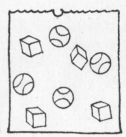

5.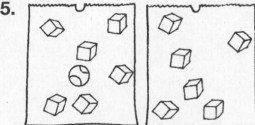

6.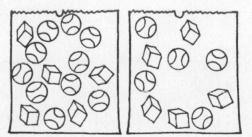

7. Circle the bag that offers an even chance of choosing a cube or a ball.

8. Circle the bag in which you would be sure of getting a cube.

 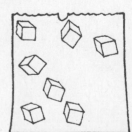

Extend Your Thinking
1-1

Critical Thinking

The Ecology Club counted all the different kinds of trees in Middletown Park. Here is their report:

Kind of Tree	Trees Counted
Oak	20
Maple	15
Willow	5
Pine	25
Birch	10

Your job is to make a pictograph of the report. Follow these steps.

1. Create a symbol.
2. Decide how many trees each symbol will represent.
3. Figure out how many symbols you need for each kind of tree in the pictograph.
4. Put each group of symbols where it belongs.
5. Make a key that shows what one symbol stands for.
6. Title your pictograph.

Check students' pictographs. Possible answers:

Trees in Middletown Park

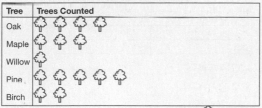

Tree	Trees Counted
Oak	
Maple	
Willow	
Pine	
Birch	

Key: = 5 trees

Use with pages 10–11. **1**

Extend Your Thinking
1-2

Critical Thinking

Your school's PTA took a survey about how much students read every day. They used the results of the survey to make this bar graph.

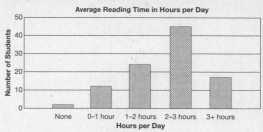

Average Reading Time in Hours per Day

Use the bar graph to decide if each statement is true or false. If it is true, write True. If it is false, write False and explain why.

1. All students read every day.
   False; About 2 students do not read every day.

2. More students read for 1–2 hours per day than 2–3 hours per day.
   False; About 24 students read for 1–2 hours per day.
   45 students read for 2–3 hours per day.

3. The largest group of students reads for 2–3 hours per day.
   True

4. Most students read for 1–3 hours each day.
   True

5. 27 students read for more than 3 hours per day.
   False; About 17 students read for more than 3 hours per day.

Extend Your Thinking
1-3

Visual Thinking

Ring the figures in each question that are exactly alike.

1.
2.
3.
4.
5.

Use with pages 14–15. **3**

Extend Your Thinking
1-4

Critical Thinking

The librarian posted the following pictograph in your school library. It shows how many books were taken out of the library each month.

Use the pictograph to answer each question.

Books Checked Out of Our Library

Month	Books Checked Out
September	
October	
November	
December	
January	

= 100 books

1. Without counting symbols, look at the pictograph and guess which month was the busiest. **January**

2. Now check your guess. Were you right? Explain.
   Possible answer: Yes; January has more symbols than any other month.

3. Suppose 600 books were checked out in February. Would the symbols used to show this data take up more space than the symbols used for September? Explain.
   Yes; September has only 5 symbols. February will have 6.

4. How many books checked out would represent? **50**

5. How many books checked out would represent? **250**

Decision Making

Angela, Ralph, and Thale are playing together. They each brought their toy car collections, but they want everyone to have the same number to play with. What should they do?

Use the bar graph to help you decide.

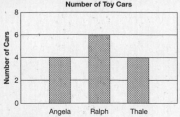

Number of Toy Cars

1. What can they do to make sure everyone has the same number of toy cars to play with?

   Possible answer: Ralph can put two of his toy cars away.

   Then everyone would have 4 cars.

2. How did you make this decision?

   Possible answer: I looked at the numbers on the graph.

   Ralph had two more cars than Angela and Thale. If he puts

   two away, he'll have the same number.

3. a. What operation did you choose to find your solution?

   Possible answer: Subtraction

   b. Write the number sentence.

   6 − 4 = 2 extra cars

4. Can you solve the problem without having to put any cars away?

   No; 14 cars cannot be shared equally by 3 people.

Patterns in Numbers

Complete each table. Then write the rule to explain changing an **In** number to an **Out** number.

1.

In	1	3	4	5	6	7
Out	2	6	8	10	12	14

Rule: **Multiply the In number by 2. Add the In number to itself.**

2.

In	1	3	5	8	4	10
Out	0	0	0	0	0	0

Rule: **Possible answer: Subtract the In number from itself.**

3.

In	1	2	3	4	5	6
Out	3	5	7	9	11	13

Rule: **Add the In number to itself plus 1.**

4.

In	12	20	35	38	54	59
Out	15	23	38	41	57	62

Rule: **Add 3.**

5.

In	12	20	35	41	49	71
Out	8	16	31	37	45	67

Rule: **Subtract 4.**

Visual Thinking

Circle the shape on the right that matches the shape on the left.

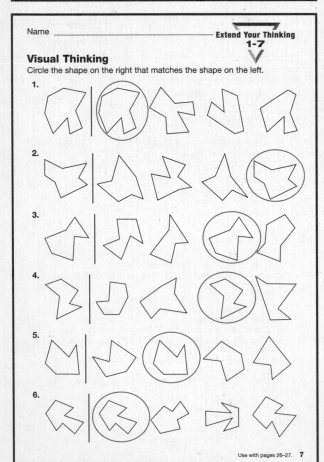

Critical Thinking

Use the pictograph to answer 1–2.

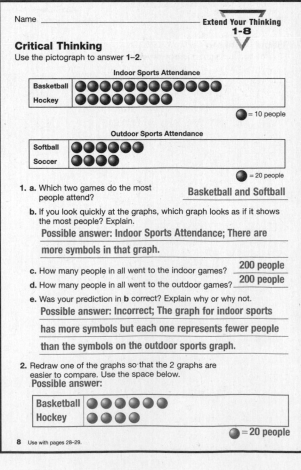

Indoor Sports Attendance

Basketball
Hockey

● = 10 people

Outdoor Sports Attendance

Softball
Soccer

● = 20 people

1. a. Which two games do the most people attend?

   Basketball and Softball

   b. If you look quickly at the graphs, which graph looks as if it shows the most people? Explain.

   Possible answer: Indoor Sports Attendance; There are

   more symbols in that graph.

   c. How many people in all went to the indoor games? **200 people**

   d. How many people in all went to the outdoor games? **200 people**

   e. Was your prediction in **b** correct? Explain why or why not.

   Possible answer: Incorrect; The graph for indoor sports

   has more symbols but each one represents fewer people

   than the symbols on the outdoor sports graph.

2. Redraw one of the graphs so that the 2 graphs are easier to compare. Use the space below.

   Possible answer:

   Basketball ● ● ● ● ● ●
   Hockey ● ● ● ●

   ● = 20 people

Visual Thinking

Circle the figure that shows the mirror image of the grid on the left.

Example:

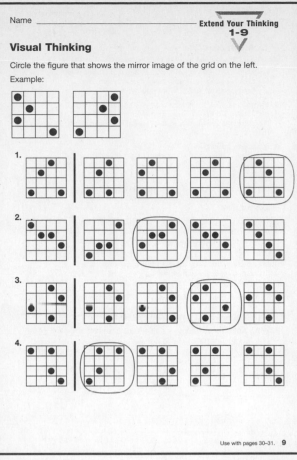

Decision Making

Your school is having a carnival. Your class wants to have a game booth to raise money for new sports equipment for the school. Your class has two choices.

Hoop Toss: Your class would set up prizes on stands and hoops for players to throw onto them. Prizes would cost $25.

Fish Bowl Toss: Your class would get some empty fish bowls and ping pong balls for players to throw into them. Prizes would cost $35.

Your class will charge $1.00 for each ticket to play a game.

To help you decide on a game, your class asked students what game they would like to play. This graph shows their votes.

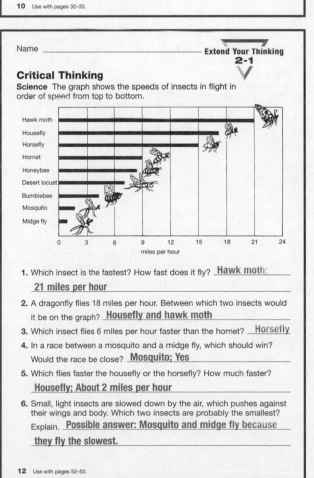

Votes for Carnival Games

| Hoop Toss | ☺ ☺ ☺ ☺ ☺ |
| Fish Bowl Toss | ☺ ☺ ☺ ☺ ☺ ☺ ☺ |

☺ = 10 students

1. Suppose everybody who voted for the hoop toss game played it once. How much money would your class make on the hoop toss?   **$45**
2. Suppose everybody who voted for the fish bowl toss played it once. How much money would your class make on the fish bowl toss?   **$65**
3. Why would you not choose a hoop toss? Explain.
   Possible answer: Not as many people would go to it.
4. Why would you not choose a fish bowl toss? Explain.
   Possible answers: Prizes cost more; It is easier to win and we might run out of prizes.
5. Which game would you choose to have? Explain.
   Possible answer: I would choose the hoop toss because it is a traditional carnival game.

Patterns in Numbers

Write numbers to complete the patterns. Then write the rule you used.

1. 2, 7, 12, 17, 22, 27, __32__, __37__, __42__
   Rule: **Add 5.**

2. 5, 10, 20, 40, __80__, __160__, __320__
   Rule: **Double the number or multiply by 2.**

3. 2, 6, 10, 14, 18, 22, 24, __26__, __30__, __34__
   Rule: **Add 4.**

4. 64, 32, 16, 8, __4__, __2__, __1__
   Rule: **Divide by 2.**

5. 7, 8, 10, 13, __17__, __22__, __28__
   Rule: **Add 1, then 2, then 3, and so on.**

6. 35, 34, 32, 29, 25, 20, __14__, __7__
   Rule: **Subtract consecutive numbers starting with 1.**

7. 100, 98, 94, 88, 80, __70__, __58__, __44__
   Rule: **Subtract consecutive even numbers starting with 2.**

8. 49, 40, 32, 25, __19__, __14__, __10__
   Rule: **Subtract 9, then 8, then 7, and so on.**

9. 36, 30, 24, 18, __12__, __6__, __0__
   Rule: **Subtract 6.**

10. 0, 9, 18, 27, __36__, __45__, __54__
    Rule: **Add 9.**

Critical Thinking

Science The graph shows the speeds of insects in flight in order of speed from top to bottom.

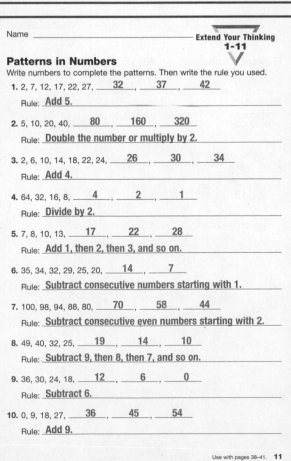

1. Which insect is the fastest? How fast does it fly? **Hawk moth; 21 miles per hour**
2. A dragonfly flies 18 miles per hour. Between which two insects would it be on the graph? **Housefly and hawk moth**
3. Which insect flies 6 miles per hour faster than the hornet? **Horsefly**
4. In a race between a mosquito and a midge fly, which should win? Would the race be close? **Mosquito; Yes**
5. Which flies faster the housefly or the horsefly? How much faster? **Housefly; About 2 miles per hour**
6. Small, light insects are slowed down by the air, which pushes against their wings and body. Which two insects are probably the smallest? Explain. **Possible answer: Mosquito and midge fly because they fly the slowest.**

Patterns in Numbers

You can use place-value rules to make number patterns.
What are the next three numbers in each pattern? Complete
the rule.

1. 10, 20, 30, 40, __50__, __60__, __70__

   Rule: Increase the number in the __tens__ place by __one__.

2. 5, 10, 15, 20, __25__, __30__, __35__

   Rule: Increase the number in the __ones__ place by __five__.

3. 100, 200, 300, 400, __500__, __600__, __700__

   Rule: Increase the number in the __hundreds__ place by __one__.

4. 35, 45, 55, 65, __75__, __85__, __95__

   Rule: Increase the number in the __tens__ place by __one__.

5. 90, 80, 70, 60, __50__, __40__, __30__

   Rule: Decrease the number in the __tens__ place by __one__.

6. 600, 500, 400, __300__, __200__, __100__

   Rule: Decrease the number in the __hundreds__ place by __one__.

7. 35, 30, 25, __20__, __15__, __10__

   Rule: Decrease the number in the __ones__ place by __five__.

8. 75, 65, 55, __45__, __35__, __25__

   Rule: Decrease the number in the __tens__ place by __one__.

Critical Thinking

Use the clues to solve the puzzles.

1. My ones digit is 4. My tens digit is 3 plus my ones digit. My hundreds digit is 7 less than my thousands digit. My thousands digit is 8. What number am I? — **8,174**

2. My ones digit is 6. My tens digit is 1 plus my ones digit. My hundreds digit is 3 less than my tens digit. My thousands digit is 3 less than my hundreds digit. What number am I? — **1,476**

3. My ones digit is 1. Add 1 to my ones digit to get my tens digit. Add 1 to my tens digit to get my hundreds digit. Add 1 to my hundreds digit to get my thousands digit. What number am I? — **4,321**

4. My thousands digit is 3. My hundreds digit is 3 − 3. My ones digit is 2. My tens digit is twice 2. What number am I? — **3,042**

5. The digit in my thousands place is 2. The digit in my ones place is 3 less than 10. The digits in the tens and hundreds places are the same. Together they add to 10. What number am I? — **2,557**

6. My ones digit and my thousands digit are the same. My tens digit is 2. My hundreds digit is 3 more than 2. My ones digit is 2 + 2. What number am I? — **4,524**

7. The digit in my thousands place is 2. The digit in my hundreds place is 2 less than 2. My tens digit is 5. My ones digit is 1 less than 5. What number am I? — **2,054**

8. Write a place-value number riddle. Give it to a classmate to solve.
   Puzzles should include place values through thousands.

   _____
   _____
   _____
   _____
   _____

Decision Making

Games Day is next week, and you're in charge of the games!
Here are some games you can play, the number of players you
need to make 2 teams, and the estimated time for each game.

> **a.** Basketball—10 players, 30 minutes
> **b.** Kickball—18 players, 15 minutes
> **c.** Indoor Soccer—10 players, 40 minutes
> **d.** Volleyball—12 players, 10 minutes

- A team may have more players than it needs, but not fewer. For example, you can have 12 players playing basketball, but not 8 players.
- Games Day lasts 4 hours.

Which games will you choose?

1. If all 4 games are played at the same time, how many players do you need? — **50 players**

2. Choose any 2 games. How many players do you need?
   Possible answers: a and b: 28 players; a and c: 20 players; a and d: 22 players; b and c: 28 players; b and d: 30 players; c and d: 22 players

3. Choose any 3 games. Which ones did you choose? How many players do you need?
   Possible answers: a, b, and c: 38 players; a, b, and d: 40 players; b, c, and d: 40 players; a, c, and d: 32 players

   _____

4. Make a schedule for Games Day. Describe how you made your choices.
   Look for answers that reflect that a team may have more players than it needs, but not less, and that take game times into consideration.

Critical Thinking

A swallowtail butterfly starts as an egg, then becomes a caterpillar. Next it enters the pupa stage, which it spends in a cocoon. Finally, it emerges as a bright yellow, red, and black butterfly!

What happens next? Use the clues to place the pictures in order from first to last.

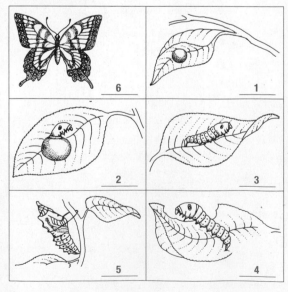

158

Critical Thinking

Animals have different life spans. They live for different lengths of time. The life spans of some animals are shown in the bar graph.

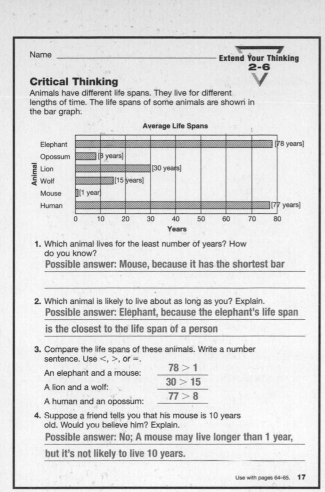

Average Life Spans

Elephant [78 years]
Opossum [8 years]
Lion [30 years]
Wolf [15 years]
Mouse [1 year]
Human [77 years]

Years

1. Which animal lives for the least number of years? How do you know?
   Possible answer: Mouse, because it has the shortest bar

2. Which animal is likely to live about as long as you? Explain.
   Possible answer: Elephant, because the elephant's life span is the closest to the life span of a person

3. Compare the life spans of these animals. Write a number sentence. Use <, >, or =.
   An elephant and a mouse: 78 > 1
   A lion and a wolf: 30 > 15
   A human and an opossum: 77 > 8

4. Suppose a friend tells you that his mouse is 10 years old. Would you believe him? Explain.
   Possible answer: No; A mouse may live longer than 1 year, but it's not likely to live 10 years.

Critical Thinking

Use the information in this chart to answer the questions.

How Deep Is the Ocean?	
Pacific Ocean	4,280 meters
Atlantic Ocean	3,635 meters
Indian Ocean	3,905 meters
Arctic Ocean	1,055 meters

1. Order the oceans by depth, from least to greatest. Describe the method you used.
   Arctic, Atlantic, Indian, Pacific; Possible answer: I wrote the names of the oceans with the least and the greatest depth, then I compared the depths of the two remaining oceans, then I wrote their names between the first two oceans, the one with the least depth first.

2. Which ocean do you think a submarine could get to the bottom of in the least amount of time? Why?
   The Arctic Ocean; It has the least depth.

3. If it takes a submarine 1 hour to dive 1,000 meters, about how long do you think it would take to reach the bottom of the Pacific Ocean? Explain your reasoning.
   Possible answer: About 4 hours because the Pacific is a little over 4,000 meters deep

4. A fish lives 3,500 meters below the surface of the water. In which oceans could this fish live?
   Atlantic, Indian, and Pacific Oceans

Patterns in Numbers

The rules of rounding can be used to list numbers.

Write the numbers that follow each rule for **1** and **2**.

1. Rounded to the nearest ten, these numbers round to 50.
   45, 46, 47, 48, 49, 50, 51, 52, 53, 54

2. Rounded to the nearest ten, these numbers round to 130.
   125, 126, 127, 128, 129, 130, 131, 132, 133, 134

3. How many whole numbers rounded to the nearest ten round to 370? Give the least and greatest numbers.
   10; 365; 374

4. How would you write a rule for rounding to hundreds?
   Possible answer: If a number is 50 or greater round to the next greater hundred; If a number is 49 or less keep the lesser hundred.

Use your rule to answer **5** and **6**.

5. If you were rounding to the nearest hundred how many numbers do you think would round to 300? Give the least and greatest number. Explain your reasoning.
   100; 250; 349; All of the numbers between and including 250 and 349 round to 300. There are 100 numbers.

6. How many numbers rounded to the nearest hundred round to 900? Give the least and greatest number.
   100; 850; 949

Visual Thinking

Read the secret code to find out these numbers.

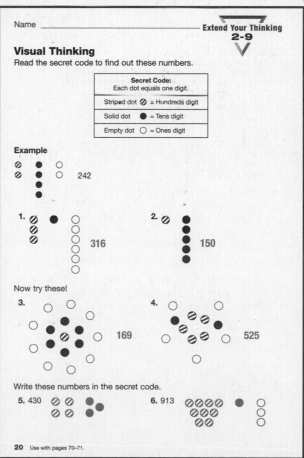

Secret Code:
Each dot equals one digit.

Striped dot ⊘ = Hundreds digit
Solid dot ● = Tens digit
Empty dot ○ = Ones digit

Example
242

1. 316
2. 150

Now try these!

3. 169
4. 525

Write these numbers in the secret code.

5. 430
6. 913

Visual Thinking

These clocks only show the numbers 3, 6, 9, and 12. Look carefully at the hands to find the time. Write the time in numbers under each clock.

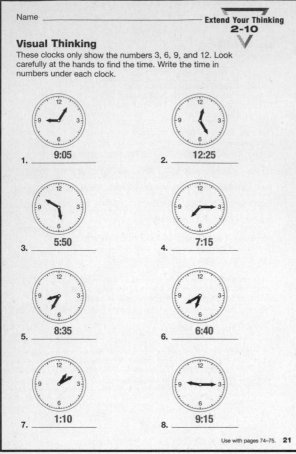

1. 9:05

2. 12:25

3. 5:50

4. 7:15

5. 8:35

6. 6:40

7. 1:10

8. 9:15

Use with pages 74–75. **21**

Critical Thinking

The Midtown Fire Department has one fire engine. One day, from 8:00 A.M. to 5:00 P.M., six calls came in at these times.

11:48 A.M.   8:28 A.M.

1:02 P.M.   4:47 P.M.

11:43 A.M.   3:18 P.M.

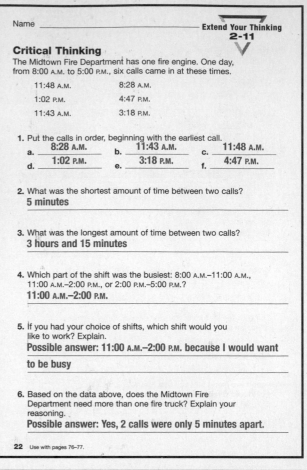

1. Put the calls in order, beginning with the earliest call.

   a. 8:28 A.M.   b. 11:43 A.M.   c. 11:48 A.M.

   d. 1:02 P.M.   e. 3:18 P.M.   f. 4:47 P.M.

2. What was the shortest amount of time between two calls?
   5 minutes

3. What was the longest amount of time between two calls?
   3 hours and 15 minutes

4. Which part of the shift was the busiest: 8:00 A.M.–11:00 A.M., 11:00 A.M.–2:00 P.M., or 2:00 P.M.–5:00 P.M.?
   11:00 A.M.–2:00 P.M.

5. If you had your choice of shifts, which shift would you like to work? Explain.
   Possible answer: 11:00 A.M.–2:00 P.M. because I would want to be busy

6. Based on the data above, does the Midtown Fire Department need more than one fire truck? Explain your reasoning.
   Possible answer: Yes, 2 calls were only 5 minutes apart.

22 Use with pages 76–77.

Visual Thinking

Lee got a new wristwatch. There's one problem. It doesn't have any numbers on it! Look at the hands and the marks on the clocks. Write the times in numbers under each watch.

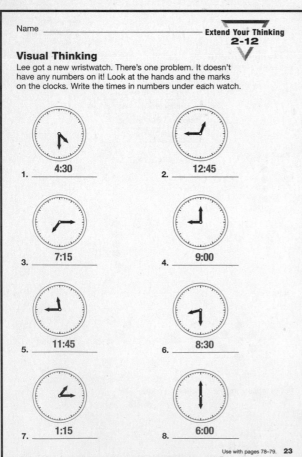

1. 4:30

2. 12:45

3. 7:15

4. 9:00

5. 11:45

6. 8:30

7. 1:15

8. 6:00

Use with pages 78–79. **23**

Decision Making

Your best friend is coming on Saturday for a visit. She will arrive at 1:00 P.M. You must be ready to take her home at 3:10 P.M. You want to do something special, so you look in the newspaper. Here's what you find:

• **Storytelling Time** begins at the library at 2:30 P.M. It will last for 45 minutes.

• **Student Concerts** begin downtown at 12:30 P.M., 2:00 P.M., and 4:30 P.M. They each last one hour.

• **A movie** begins at 1:45 P.M. and runs for two hours and ten minutes.

• **A karate demonstration** begins at your school at 1:30. It will last for an hour and a half.

1. What time will the Storytelling Time end?   **3:15 P.M.**

2. What time will each concert end?
   1:30 P.M. , **3:00 P.M.** , and **5:30 P.M.** .

3. What time will the movie end?   **3:55 P.M.**

4. What time will the karate demonstration end?   **3:00 P.M.**

5. Which activities will you and your friend have time for?
   The 2:00 concert or the karate demonstration

6. Which activity would you choose? Why?
   Answers will vary.

24 Use with pages 80–81.

Critical Thinking

Your class wants to add some new holidays to the calendar!

Use the calendar below to find the date for each holiday listed below. Write the date next to each holiday's name.

1. Pet Day: the first Friday in June: _June 6th_

2. Best Friend Day: the third Monday in October: _October 20th_

3. Pizza Day: the fourth Tuesday in July: _July 22nd_

4. Pen-Pal Day: the second Wednesday in September: _September 10th_

5. Exercise Day: the third Friday in November: _November 21st_

6. Hat Day: the first Thursday in August: _August 7th_

7. Your Own Holiday: the fifth Monday in September: _September 29th_

Decision Making

You're in charge of making a schedule for the Pet Club meeting. Here is the list of activities for the meeting.

- Announcements _____
- Dr. Evans talks about "Your Pets' Teeth." __20 minutes__
- Roberto shows his pet guinea pig. _____
- Jody shows her pet iguana. _____
- Samantha shows her pet tarantula. _____

The meeting will begin at 4:00 P.M. and end at 5:00 P.M.

1. How much time do you have? _One hour_

2. Dr. Evans, the vet, needs 20 minutes. How much time will each of the other activities take? Write your estimates next to each activity.

Answers will vary, but average time for each remaining activity is 10 minutes.

3. Make a schedule for the meeting. Write it in the chart.

Possible answer:

Pet Club Meeting	
Time	Activity
4:00 P.M.	Announcements
4:10 P.M.	Dr. Evans
4:30 P.M.	Roberto
4:40 P.M.	Jody
4:50 P.M.	Samantha

4. Compare your schedule with one or two friends. How are the schedules different?

Answers will vary.

Patterns in Algebra

Basic facts and place-value patterns can help you add greater numbers.

Use patterns to help you fill in the blanks.

1. 60 + _70_ = 130

2. _90_ + 30 = 120

3. 40 + 60 = _100_

4. 60 + _50_ = 110

5. _600_ + 700 = 1,300

6. 50 + _70_ = 120

7. 900 + _300_ = 1,200

8. _60_ + 30 = 90

9. _400_ + 300 = 700

10. _400_ + 600 = 1,000

11. 700 + 900 = _1,600_

12. 600 + 500 = _1,100_

13. 500 + 700 = _1,200_

14. 40 + 30 = _70_

15. 600 + _300_ = 900

16. _70_ + 90 = 160

17. 400 + _500_ = 900

18. 70 + _70_ = 140

19. _70_ + 80 = 150

20. _200_ + 300 = 500

21. 600 + _800_ = 1,400

22. 90 + _90_ = 180

23. 50 + _80_ = 130

24. 20 + _90_ = 110

25. _800_ + 400 = 1,200

26. 700 + _200_ = 900

27. _700_ + 400 = 1,100

28. _600_ + 900 = 1,500

29. 300 + _800_ = 1,100

30. _200_ + 700 = 900

31. _600_ + 400 = 1,000

32. _900_ + 900 = 1,800

Critical Thinking

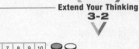

1	2	3	4	5	6	7	8	9	10
11	12	13	14	15	16	17	18	19	20
21	22	23	24	25	26	27	28	29	30
31	32	33	34	35	36	37	38	39	40
41	42	43	44	45	46	47	48	49	50
51	52	53	54	55	56	57	58	59	60
61	62	63	64	65	66	67	68	69	70
71	72	73	74	75	76	77	78	79	80
81	82	83	84	85	86	87	88	89	90
91	92	93	94	95	96	97	98	99	100

Beth and Seth are playing a game. They each put a counter on the hundreds chart.

1. Beth says, "If you go over 2 spaces to the right and up 3 rows from my number, you will be at 27. What is my number?" Explain your reasoning.

55; Start at 27, go over 2 spaces to the left and down 3 rows.

2. Seth says, "If you go over 3 spaces to the left and down 2 rows from my number, you will be at 85. What is my number?" Explain your reasoning.

68; Start at 85, go over 3 spaces to the right and up 2 rows.

3. Beth says, "If you go over to the right 4 spaces from my number, you will move into the 70's row for the last 2 spaces. What is my number?" Explain your reasoning.

68; 4 spaces to the right of 68 brings you to the end of the 60's and 2 into the 70s is 72.

4. Seth says, "From my number, go up 2 rows and over to the left 3 spaces. You will be at 39. What's my number?" Explain your reasoning.

62; go down 2 rows from 39 and to the right 3 spaces (which turns a row).

Visual Thinking

Name _____

Choose the shape that can be added to the first shape to make the second shape. Circle your choice.

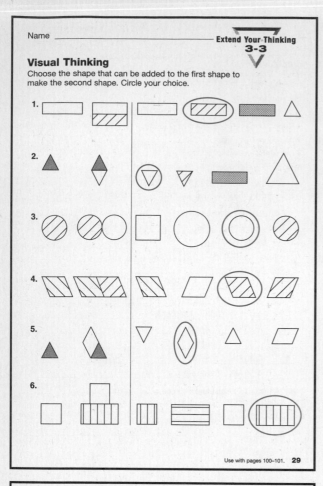

Decision Making

Your Little League team wants to buy new uniforms and new equipment. There are 18 players on your team. Your coach has created a list with packages of different items and their costs. However, the team will only buy 2 packages on the list.

Packages of:	Total Cost
18 baseball caps	$63
2 dozen t-shirts	$76
18 pairs of socks	$24
18 sweatshirts	$81
6 baseballs	$39
4 bats	$45

1. a. What are the 2 most expensive packages on the list?
   The t-shirts and the sweatshirts

   b. About how much is their total cost? **$160**

2. a. Which 2 packages on the list could be purchased for about $65?
   Possible answers: socks and the baseballs; socks and bats

   b. What are their total costs? Possible answers: $63; $69

3. There are other things besides cost to consider when making your decision. What questions would you ask to help you choose the two packages? List two questions below. Possible answers:

   Question 1: What is the condition of your team's clothing?

   Question 2: Does your team need more bats and balls?

4. Do you have enough information to make a decision? Explain.
   Possible answer: No; until I get answers to my questions,
   I don't have enough information to make a decision.

5. Choose two packages to buy. Tell how much they cost and why you chose them.
   Possible answer: Socks and t-shirts; $100.
   Ours were worn out.

Critical Thinking

Here is a list of some of the tallest buildings in Cleveland, Ohio.

Tallest Buildings in Cleveland, Ohio	
Building	**Number of Stories**
Society Center	57
Terminal Tower	52
Bank One Center	28
Federal Building	32
J.A. Rhodes Tower	23
Ohio-Bell	22

1. a. What is the total number of stories in the Society Center and the J.A. Rhodes Tower? **80 stories**

   b. How did you find the answer?
   I added 57 + 23 and regrouped 10 ones for 1 ten.

   c. How can you check your answer?
   I could estimate the sum of 57 + 23. The estimate is 80.

2. Suppose the owners of the Ohio-Bell building decide to add 19 stories to the building and the owners of the Bank One Center decide to add 24 stories to their building. After construction, which building will be the tallest in the list? Explain.
   The Society Center; 22 + 19 = 41 stories in the new
   Ohio-Bell building, 28 + 24 = 52 stories in the new
   Bank One Center, the Society Center is still the tallest
   building with 57 stories.

Critical Thinking

Joanie writes in a journal where she keeps track of how much she reads each day for different subjects in school and for fun.

> **Monday**
> 10 pages – Social Studies
> 15 pages – Reading
> 7 pages – Math
> 22 pages – My library book
> **Tuesday**
> 17 pages – Science
> 29 pages – Reading
> 6 pages – Math
> 14 pages – My library book
> **Wednesday**
> 23 pages – Social Studies
> 18 pages – Science
> 9 pages – Math
> 7 pages – My library book
> **Thursday**
> **Friday**
> **Saturday**

1. How many total pages has Joanie read for science class?
   35 pages

2. How many pages did Joanie read in all on Monday?
   54 pages

3. What is the total number of pages Joanie read for social studies?
   33 pages

4. Joanie has to read 40 pages for science this week.

   a. How many more pages does Joanie have to read? **5 pages**

   b. What strategy did you use to solve the problem? Possible answer:
   Choose an Operation or Use Logical Reasoning.

   c. How many pages for science could Joanie read on Thursday and Friday to meet her goal? Possible answer: She could read 2 pages on Thursday and 3 on Friday.

5. On Sunday, Joanie had 100 pages left to read in her library book.

   a. How many pages does she have to read now? **57 pages**

   b. The library book is due on Saturday. How many pages could Joanie read on Thursday and Friday so that she completes the book?
   Answers will vary. Sum of pages read on Thursday and
   Friday should be 57.

Visual Thinking

A group of students found this paper in the gym. It shows addition problems written in code. The table gives some information about the code. Use the table to crack the code. Then solve the problems. Be sure to use the code to give your answers!

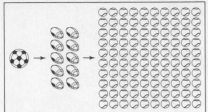

Write a number sentence and find the sum for each.

1.
$453 + 227 = 680$

2.
$526 + 375 = 901$

3.
$189 + 624 = 813$

4.
$312 + 409 = 721$

Patterns in Numbers

What are the next three numbers? Tell what rule was used to make the pattern.

1. 1,550; 1,650; 1,750; 1,850; __1,950__ ; __2,050__ ; __2,150__
   Rule: __Add 100 to the previous number.__

2. 3,120; 3,270; 3,420; 3,570; __3,720__ ; __3,870__ ; __4,020__
   Rule: __Add 150 to the previous number.__

3. 4,600; 5,200; 5,900; 6,700; __7,600__ ; __8,600__ ; __9,700__
   Rule: __Add successive 100's: 600, 700, 800, . . . 1,100.__

4. 149; 298; 596; 1,192; __2,384__ ; __4,768__ ; __9,536__
   Rule: __Double the previous number.__

5. 452; 563; 785; 1,118; __1,562__ ; __2,117__ ; __2,783__
   Rule: __Add successive 3-same-digit numbers:__
   __111, 222, 333, . . . 666.__

6. 1,239; 1,564; 1,989; 2,514; __3,139__ ; __3,864__ ; __4,689__
   Rule: __Add successive numbers: 325, 425, 525, . . . 825.__

7. 234; 334; 534; 834; __1,234__ ; __1,734__ ; __2,334__
   Rule: __Add successive 100s: 100, 200, 300, . . . 600.__

Decision Making

The Science Club has collected 192 rock samples. The rocks need to be classified according to similar traits. Club members observed the rocks. They made this chart.

Trait	Number of Rocks
Light colored, round edges, leaves a streak	22
Dark colored, round edges, leaves a streak	18
Light colored, sharp edges, leaves a streak	17
Dark colored, sharp edges, leaves a streak	29
Light colored, round edges, no streak	16
Dark colored, round edges, no streak	44
Light colored, sharp edges, no streak	20
Dark colored, sharp edges, no streak	26

Club members have decided to use egg cartons to hold their rocks. They can place up to 12 rocks in each egg carton.

1. The club could classify the rocks as either light or dark colored. If they use this plan, how many egg cartons would be needed to hold the light colored rocks? The dark colored?
   __7 for the light colored, 10 for the dark colored__

2. The club could classify the rocks as those with round edges leaving a streak, with round edges leaving no streak, with sharp edges leaving a streak, and with sharp edges leaving no streak. If they use this plan, how many egg cartons would be needed to hold each group?
   __Round, streak = 4; round, no streak = 5;__
   __Sharp, streak = 4; sharp, no streak = 4__

3. How do you think the club should classify the rocks? Create a classification system for the club. Describe it below.
   __Possible answers: Light, sharp edges (37); light, round edges__
   __(38); dark, sharp edges (55); dark, round edges (62)__

Critical Thinking

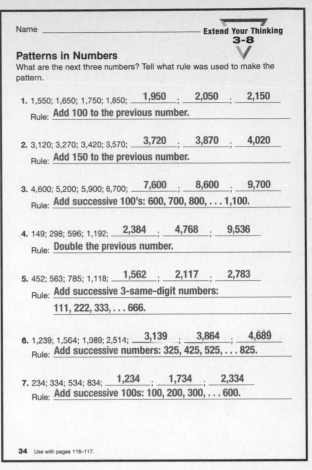

1.
These are clanks.   These are not clanks.
How are all clanks alike?
__Formed from a triangle__

2.
These are kwumps.   These are not kwumps.
How are all kwumps alike?
__Formed from a rectangle__

3.
These are brips.   These are not brips.
How are all brips alike?
__Formed from two connecting triangles__

4.
Which of these is a
a. clank? __D__   b. kwump? __C__   c. brip? __A__

5. In the box below, draw a clank, kwump, and brip.
   __Check students' answers.__

clank	kwump	brip

**Extend Your Thinking
3-11**

Patterns in Numbers

Use mental math to find the next three numbers in each pattern.
Tell what rule was used to make the pattern.

1. 11, 21, 31, 41, ___51___, ___61___, ___71___
   Rule: Add 10.

2. 25, 38, 51, 64, ___77___, ___90___, ___103___
   Rule: Add 13.

3. 17, 33, 49, 65, ___81___, ___97___, ___113___
   Rule: Add 16.

4. 24, 44, 64, 84, ___104___, ___124___, ___144___
   Rule: Add 20.

5. 11, 20, 29, 38, ___47___, ___56___, ___65___
   Rule: Add 9.

6. 11, 32, 53, 74, ___95___, ___116___, ___137___
   Rule: Add 21.

7. 48, 64, 80, 96, ___112___, ___128___, ___144___
   Rule: Add 16.

8. 16, 58, 100, ___142___, ___184___, ___226___
   Rule: Add 42.

**Extend Your Thinking
3-12**

Critical Thinking

Three coins used in the United States during the 1800's are
shown below. The value of each of these coins was greater
than $1.00!

$10 $20 $50

Eagle   Double Eagle $50 Gold Piece

1. How many eagles equals one $50 gold piece? How do
   you know?
   5; $10 + $10 + $10 + $10 + $10 = $50

2.    3.

   What is the total value of
   these coins? **$80**

   What is the total value of
   these coins? **$60**

4. Describe how you found the total value of the coins in **2** and **3**.
   Possible answer: I counted each coin.

5. Find four ways to make $100.00.
   Possible answer: Two $50 gold pieces; one $50 gold piece
   and 5 eagles; 10 eagles; 5 double eagles.

6. Each of these coins was replaced with paper money.
   Why do you think this change was made? **Possible answer:**
   Paper money is lighter and easier to produce.

**Extend Your Thinking
3-13**

Critical Thinking

Your class is holding a coin collection display. Three
students bring in their collection. You have 4 quarters,
7 dimes, 5 nickels, and 10 pennies. José has 6 quarters,
5 dimes, 3 nickels, and 7 pennies. Margaret has 3 quarters,
4 dimes, 8 nickels, and 10 pennies.

1. How many coins are there in each collection?
   a. yours ___26___   b. José's ___21___   c. Margaret's ___25___

2. What is the total value of each collection?
   a. yours ___$2.05___   b. José's ___$2.22___   c. Margaret's ___$1.65___

3. Here is a bar graph of your coin collection. Add bars to
   the graph to show José's and Margaret's coin collections.

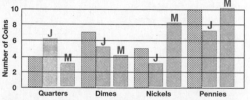

4. Is the coin collection with the greatest number of coins
   also the one with greatest value? Why?
   No; The collection with the greatest value has the least
   number of coins. The total value depends on the value of
   each individual coin.

**Extend Your Thinking
3-14**

Critical Thinking

Your music class is having a bake
sale to raise money for new
instruments. You are the cashier.
You start with 3 one-dollar bills,
12 quarters, 10 dimes, 10 nickels,
and 15 pennies in the cash register.

Price List	
oatmeal cookie	$0.76
apple pie	$3.82
muffin	$1.39
strawberry shortcake	$2.99

1. How much money is in the cash register? ___$7.65___

2. Jim is first in line. He buys a muffin with $5.00.
   a. How much change will you give Jim? ___$3.61___
   b. Which bills and coins will you use?
      3 one-dollar bills, 2 quarters, 1 dime, 1 penny
   c. Which bills and coins are in the cash register now?
      1 five-dollar bill, 10 quarters, 9 dimes, 10 nickels,
      14 pennies

2. Lucia is second in line. She buys an apple pie with $5.00.
   a. How much change will you give her? ___$1.18___
   b. Which bills and coins will you use? (Remember, you have different
      bills and coins in the cash register now!)
      4 quarters, 1 dime, 1 nickel, 3 pennies
   c. Which bills and coins are in the cash register now?
      2 five-dollar bills, 6 quarters, 8 dimes, 9 nickels,
      11 pennies

3. If a customer gave you a five-dollar bill to pay for a piece of
   strawberry shortcake, would you be able to make change? Explain.
   Yes, you could give the customer 6 quarters, 5 dimes,
   and 1 penny.

Patterns in Numbers

Continue each pattern. Write the next three numbers using dollars and cents or just cents. Then write the rule.

1. 12¢, 22¢, 32¢, 42¢, __52¢__, __62¢__, __72¢__
   Rule: __Add 10¢.__

2. $0.55, $0.80, $1.05, $1.30, __$1.55__, __$1.80__, __$2.05__
   Rule: __Add $0.25.__

3. 36¢, 42¢, 48¢, 54¢, __60¢__, __66¢__, __72¢__
   Rule: __Add 6¢.__

4. $0.89, $2.14, $3.39, $4.64, __$5.89__, __$7.14__, __$8.39__
   Rule: __Add $1.25.__

5. 109¢, 251¢, 393¢, 535¢, __677¢__, __819¢__, __961¢__
   Rule: __Add 142¢.__

6. $1.99, $2.07, $2.15, $2.23, __$2.31__, __$2.39__, __$2.47__
   Rule: __Add $0.08.__

7. $0.12, $1.13, $2.14, $3.15, __$4.16__, __$5.17__, __$6.18__
   Rule: __Add $1.01.__

8. 15¢, 57¢, 99¢, 141¢, __183¢__, __225¢__, __267¢__
   Rule: __Add 42¢.__

9. $0.03, $2.02, $4.01, $6.00, __$7.99__, __$9.98__, __$11.97__
   Rule: __Add $1.99.__

10. 5¢, 22¢, 39¢, 56¢, __73¢__, __90¢__, __107¢__
    Rule: __Add 17¢.__

Decision Making

On Saturday you are going to spend the day with your 5-year-old sister and your aunt. You plan to choose a fun place to visit. Together you have $18.00 to spend.

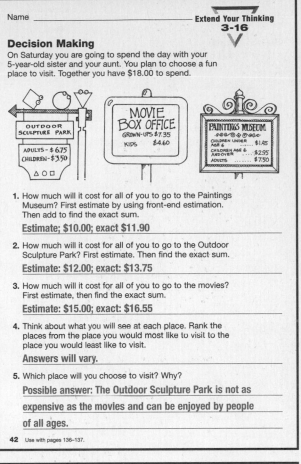

1. How much will it cost for all of you to go to the Paintings Museum? First estimate by using front-end estimation. Then add to find the exact sum.
   __Estimate; $10.00; exact $11.90__

2. How much will it cost for all of you to go to the Outdoor Sculpture Park? First estimate. Then find the exact sum.
   __Estimate: $12.00; exact: $13.75__

3. How much will it cost for all of you to go to the movies? First estimate, then find the exact sum.
   __Estimate: $15.00; exact: $16.55__

4. Think about what you will see at each place. Rank the places from the place you would most like to visit to the place you would least like to visit.
   __Answers will vary.__

5. Which place will you choose to visit? Why?
   __Possible answer: The Outdoor Sculpture Park is not as__
   __expensive as the movies and can be enjoyed by people__
   __of all ages.__

Decision Making

You've just given your dog a bath in your bathtub and it made quite a mess. You are going to the hardware store to buy supplies to clean the bathroom. You have $15.00 to spend. You find a mop for $6.63, liquid soap for $1.89, a broom for $4.12, paper towels for $1.19 and a pack of sponges for $3.27.

1. List three items you can purchase with $15.00.
   __Possible answers: mop, liquid soap, and broom; mop, broom,__
   __and sponges; paper towels, sponges, and broom__

2. Which two items do you think would be the most important to buy? Why?
   __Possible answers: sponges and mop because there is a lot of__
   __water to clean up; liquid soap and sponges to clean the bathtub__

3. Which two items do you think would be the least important to buy? Why?
   __Possible answer: paper towels and broom because they__
   __won't help clean up the water very well__

4. Which items would you purchase to clean the bathroom without going over $15.00?
   __Possible answer: paper towels, sponges, broom, and__
   __liquid soap__

5. What is the total cost of your purchase?
   __Check students' answers.__

6. How much change would you receive from $15.00?
   __Check students' answers.__

7. Describe how you made your choices.
   __Check students' answers.__

Visual Thinking

Circle the animal in each row that is different.

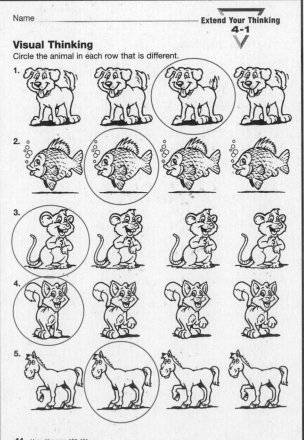

165

Extend Your Thinking
4-2

Critical Thinking

A stationery store is planning to have a grand opening. In order to attract customers, the store is going to give away free pencils.

The store manager needs to keep track of how many pencils are given out, so that she can get more when needed. She starts off with 1,000 pencils in stock. Every hour, she checks her supply.

Use subtraction and addition patterns to complete the table.

Each picture of a pencil on the chart represents 100 pencils. Write your answers in numbers.

	Time	Pencils Given Away	Pencils Re-Stocked	Pencils in Stock
1.	9:00 A.M.	none	none	1,000
2.	10:00 A.M.	🖊🖊🖊	none	700
3.	11:00 A.M.	🖊🖊🖊🖊🖊	none	200
4.	12:00 A.M.	🖊🖊	🖊🖊🖊🖊🖊	500
5.	1:00 P.M.	🖊🖊🖊🖊	🖊🖊🖊🖊🖊🖊	700
6.	2:00 P.M.	🖊🖊🖊	🖊🖊	600
7.	3:00 P.M.	🖊🖊	none	400
8.	4:00 P.M.	🖊	🖊🖊	500
9.	5:00 P.M.	none	none	500

10. How many pencils did the manager give away in total?

__2,000__

Extend Your Thinking
4-3

Patterns in Numbers

All of the third-graders at the Dorset Elementary School are working hard to raise money for new equipment for the school playground. The Community Parks Committee has volunteered to donate $100 for every $10 that the students raise. The goal is to raise $3,000. Use the chart below to see how they meet their goal.

	Week 1	Week 2	Week 3
Money Raised by Students	$40	$250	$60
Contribution	$400	$2,500	$600

1. In which week do the students meet their goal? __Second week__

2. What is the total contribution made by the Parks Committee?
__$3,500__

3. How much money do the students raise on their own?
__$350__

4. How much money was raised all together? __$3,850__

5. Suppose the students raised $100 in the second week. Create a new chart that shows how the students could meet their goal in 5 weeks.

Possible answer:

	Week 1	Week 2	Week 3	Week 4	Week 5
Money Raised by Students	$40	$100	$60	$50	$50
Contribution	$400	$1,000	$600	$500	$500

Extend Your Thinking
4-4

Patterns in Numbers

A ☆☆☆ ☆☆☆   B ☆☆☆☆ ☆☆☆☆   C ☆☆☆☆☆☆☆☆ ☆☆☆☆☆☆☆☆   D   E

1. How many stars should be in box D in order to continue the pattern?
__48; (24 + 24)__

2. About how many stars should be in box E? __About 100; (50 + 50)__

3. What is the exact amount of stars that should be in box E?
__96; (48 + 48)__

4. Explain the rule for this pattern.
__The number of stars doubles each time.__

Make a list or choose any strategy to answer the questions.

5. a. If the pattern continued which box would be the first to have more than 1,000 stars? __I__

   b. Which box would be the first to have more than 5,000 stars? __K__

6. Fill in boxes D and E with the correct number of triangles.

A △△△△△ △△△△△ △△△△△ △△△△△   B △△△△△ △△△△△ △△△△△ △△△△   C △△△△△ △△△△△ △△△△△ △△△   D △△△△△ △△△△△ △△   E △△△△△ △△△△

7. Explain the rule for this pattern.
__Subtract 4 triangles each time.__

Extend Your Thinking
4-5

Critical Thinking

Imagine that you live in a country where the people use knives, forks and spoons for money! Spoons have the least value. They have a value of 1. Forks are worth more. They are worth 10 spoons. Knives have the most value. Each knife is worth 100 spoons.

1. Use the information below to figure out the amount shown.

__111__ spoons

2. Suppose you are shopping in this country. You want to buy something that costs 4 knives, 6 forks. You have only 3 knives and 17 forks.

   a. How can you make your purchase? Explain.
   __Give 3 knives and 16 forks to the seller.__

   b. How much will you have left? __1 fork__

3. You want to buy something for 1 knife, 6 forks, 4 spoons. You give the seller 2 knives. What will your change be?
__Possible answer: 3 forks, 6 spoons__

4. You buy two items; one for 3 knives, 4 forks, 7 spoons, and one for 4 knives, 7 forks, 8 spoons. What is the total cost of your purchase? Write it in the least number of knives, forks and spoons possible.
__8 knives, 2 forks, 5 spoons__

5. Write your own problem using knives, forks and spoons as money. Share it with a friend.
__Answers will vary; Check students' problems.__

Worksheet 4-6 (page 49)

Name _____

Critical Thinking

The amount of time animals need to carry their young until they are born can vary greatly. Use the information below to answer the questions.

Cats	63 days	Mice	20 days
Dogs	61 days	Rabbits	31 days
Foxes	52 days	Squirrels	44 days
Guinea Pigs	68 days	Wolves	63 days
Kangaroos	42 days		

1. Would you say a rabbit needs about a month for its young to be born? Explain.

   Yes; 31 days is the same as a month.

2. Would you say a kangaroo and a squirrel need about the same amount of time? Explain.

   Yes; 42 and 44 are close enough to be called "about the same."

3. About how many months do cats and wolves need? Explain.

   Cats and wolves need about 2 months; If a month has 31 days, 63 days is just one more day than 2 months.

4. List the animals that need more than one month but less than 2 months.

   Foxes, kangaroos, and squirrels

5. List the animals that need about 6 weeks. Explain.

   Kangaroos and squirrels; 6 weeks is 42 days.

6. Which animal needs only about 3 weeks? Explain.

   Mice; 3 weeks is 21 days, and 20 days is close enough to be called "about 3 weeks."

Worksheet 4-7 (page 50)

Name _____

Critical Thinking

Lizette wants to exchange her coins, but she doesn't have enough. Write the amount of money she needs to exchange for the amount shown.

1. Lizette needs __**8¢**__ to exchange the coins for 25¢.

2. Lizette needs __**9¢**__ to exchange the coins for 50¢.

3. Lizette needs __**18¢**__ to exchange the coins for $1.00.

4. Lizette needs __**8¢**__ to exchange the coins for $1.00.

5. Lizette needs __**32¢**__ to exchange the coins for $2.00.

6. Lizette needs __**56¢**__ to exchange the coins for $5.00.

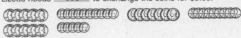

7. Describe how you found the amount of money Lizette needed.

   Possible answer: Count the change and subtract from the amount shown.

Worksheet 4-8 (page 51)

Name _____

Patterns in Numbers

Write the next 3 numbers in each pattern. Then write the rule you used to complete the pattern.

1. 190, 180, 170, __160__, __150__, __140__

   Rule: **Subtract 10.**

2. 240, 220, 200, __180__, __160__, __140__

   Rule: **Subtract 20.**

3. 10, 40, 70, __100__, __130__, __160__

   Rule: **Add 30.**

4. 50, 100, 150, __200__, __250__, __300__

   Rule: **Add 50.**

5. 195, 180, 165, __150__, __135__, __120__

   Rule: **Subtract 15.**

6. 178, 169, 160, __151__, __142__, __133__

   Rule: **Subtract 9.**

7. 204, 191, 178, __165__, __152__, __139__

   Rule: **Subtract 13.**

8. 107, 142, 177, __212__, __247__, __282__

   Rule: **Add 35.**

9. 935, 811, 687, __563__, __439__, __315__

   Rule: **Subtract 124.**

10. 849, 695, 541, __387__, __233__, __79__

    Rule: **Subtract 154.**

11. 500, 467, 434, 401, __368__, __335__, __302__

    Rule: **Subtract 33.**

Worksheet 4-9 (page 52)

Name _____

Visual Thinking

Look at the two shapes on the left in each row. Imagine that the smaller shape is cut out of the larger shape. Circle the shape on the right that shows the remaining cut shape.

1.
   a.   b.   c.   d.

2.
   a.   b.   c.   d.

3.
   a.   b.   c.   d.

4.
   a.   b.   c.   d.

5.
   a.   b.   c.   d.

Critical Thinking

North America has many different rivers running through it. In fact, rivers can be longer than some states! Here are some rivers which run through North America. Use the table to answer the questions.

River	Where it Starts	Length in Miles
Cumberland	Kentucky	720
Yellowstone	Wyoming	692
Ohio-Allegheny	Pennsylvania	981
Tombigbee	Mississippi	525
Liard	Alaska	693
Brazos	Texas	923
Sacramento	California	377

1. What is the difference in length between the longest river and the shortest river? __604 miles__

2. If you drive straight across from one side of Colorado to the other, you will have driven approximately 385 miles. How much longer would you have to drive to cover the entire length of the Brazos river? Explain.

   __538 miles; The Brazos river is 923 miles long;__

   __923 − 385 = 538 miles.__

3. Felicia likes to go white-water rafting on rivers across North America. If she travels 120 miles each day, how many days will it take her to raft the entire length of the Cumberland river?

   a. Make a table at the right to help you find the answer. Use the headings "Number of days" and "Number of miles" in each column.

   b. How many days will it take Felicia to raft the Cumberland river?

   __6 days__

Rafting the Cumberland	
Number of Days	Number of Miles
1	120
2	240
3	360
4	480
5	600
6	720

Decision Making

Lynn's goal for her summer vacation is to read a total of 500 pages. So far, she has read 383 pages. She has time to read one more book before the end of the summer. She has narrowed down her book choices to 3 books from her local library.

Book A: *The Wonderful World of Bugs*—134 pages

Book B: *The Summer Dance*—122 pages

Book C: *Scary Tales of Lore*—140 pages

1. How many more pages does Lynn need to read to reach her goal of 500 pages? __117__

2. Will each of the books allow Lynn to reach her goal? Write yes or no.

   Book A __Yes__   Book B __Yes__   Book C __Yes__

3. How many pages over or under her goal will Lynn read for each book choice?

   Book A __17 over__   Book B __5 over__   Book C __23 over__

4. Look at each book's title. What do you think each book is about? Explain. **Possible answers:**

   Book A: __The book might be about insects.__

   Book B: __The book might be about a summer dance.__

   Book C: __The book might be about scary stories.__

5. Which book do you think Lynn should read? Why?

   __Possible answer: Lynn should read Book C because it would__

   __be enjoyable to read, and she would read the most pages__

   __past her goal.__

Patterns in Numbers

Use patterns to help you fill in the blanks.

1. $7 − 4 =$ __3__
   $70 − 40 =$ __30__
   $700 − 400 =$ __300__
   $7,000 − 4,000 =$ __3,000__

2. __800__ $− 200 = 600$
   $8 −$ __2__ $= 6$
   $80 − 20 =$ __60__
   __8,000__ $− 2,000 = 6,000$

3. $9 − 3 =$ __6__
   $90 −$ __30__ $= 60$
   $900 − 300 =$ __600__
   __9,000__ $− 3,000 = 6,000$

4. $1,200 −$ __500__ $= 700$
   $120 − 50 =$ __70__
   __12__ $− 5 = 7$

5. $150 − 80 =$ __70__
   $15 −$ __8__ $= 7$
   __1,500__ $− 800 = 700$

6. $23 − 14 =$ __9__
   $230 −$ __140__ $= 90$
   __2,300__ $− 1,400 = 900$

7. $60 −$ __10__ $= 50$
   $6,000 − 1,000 =$ __5,000__
   __600__ $− 100 = 500$
   $6 − 1 =$ __5__

8. $340 − 170 =$ __170__
   $3,400 − 1,700 =$ __1,700__
   __34__ $− 17 = 17$
   $34,000 −$ __17,000__ $= 17,000$

Complete the patterns. Write the rule for each.

9. $6,543; 6,366; 6,189;$ __6,012__ ; __5,835__

   Rule: __Subtract 177.__

10. $5,709; 5,654;$ __5,599__ , __5,544__ ; __5,489__

    Rule: __Subtract 55.__

Critical Thinking

Mrs. Lyons baked 85 loaves of bread for the school bake sale. The sale ran for 3 days. On the first day, Monday, 35 loaves were sold. At the end of the second day, there were 25 left. On the third day, 14 more were sold. Mrs. Lyons will receive a prize from the bake sale committee if she sells at least 70 loaves.

1. How many loaves were sold on:

   a. Monday? __35__

   b. Tuesday? __25__

   c. Wednesday? __14__

2. How many loaves did Mrs. Lyons sell all together? __74 loaves__

3. Did Mrs. Lyons sell all the bread she made? __No__

4. Will Mrs. Lyons win the prize? __Yes__

5. Did Mrs. Lyons have to sell any bread at all on Wednesday in order to win the prize? Explain.

   __Possible answer: Yes, she needed to sell at least 10 loaves.__

6. If Mrs. Lyons had sold only 20 loaves on Tuesday, would she have sold enough to win the prize? How do you know?

   __No; Possible answer: 35 + 20 + 14 = 69, she would have__

   __been short by 1 loaf of bread.__

7. Mrs. Lyons decided to sell bread on Thursday until she sold all that was left. How many loaves does Mrs. Lyons have to sell?

   __11 loaves__

8. Mrs. Lyons baked muffins for the next bake sale, which ran for 4 days. If she needed to sell 75 muffins to win a prize and she sold about the same number each day, about how many would she have to sell each day?

   __About 20 muffins__

Worksheet 4-14 (top left)

Decision Making

Roberto, Michael and Stephanie are planning a route for a bike-a-thon. The bike ride will start and finish at the park.

Use the map and the following information to plan a route.

- The route should be 15 to 20 blocks long.
- The route must pass the library, the school and the bookstore.
- Bikers are not allowed to ride on the same block more than once.

1. Draw your route on the map. Explain why you chose the route you did.
   Check students' routes.

2. If Roberto wanted to ride from home to Michael's house and pass by Stephanie's house on the way, what are the least number of blocks he would have to ride?
   6 blocks

3. Using a different colored pencil, draw a route around as many blocks as you can without riding on the same stretch of road twice. **Check students' answers.**

Worksheet 4-15 (top right)

Critical Thinking
Find the missing digits.

1. $15 – $__6__ = $9

2. $27 – $__14__ = $13

3. $__58__ – $26 = $32

4. $__101__ – $47 = $54

5. $37 – $__13__ = $24

6. $__91__ – $81 = $10

7. $4.32 – $__3.13__ = $1.19

8. $10.00 – $__6.84__ = $3.16

9. $__8.83__ – $1.21 = $7.62

10. $__19.82__ – $6.21 = $13.61

11. $__28.42__ – $8.42 = $20.00

12. $15.00 – $__5.21__ = $9.79

13.
```
  $ 4 . 4 9
-   1 . 8 4
  $ 2 . 6 5
```

14.
```
  $ 2 0 . 7 8
-     6 . 4 9
  $ 1 4 . 2 9
```

15.
```
  $ 1 5 . 1 7
-     9 . 4 1
  $   5 . 7 6
```

16. Describe the method you used to find the missing digits.
    Possible answers: Used basic facts; subtracted pairs of digits.

17. Karen has $10. She buys one item for $1.74 and another for $2.29.

    a. How much does she spend? **$4.03**

    b. How much change will she get from a $5 bill?
    97¢

    c. Does she have enough money left for 3 items costing $2.03 each? Explain.
    No; She needs another 12¢.

Worksheet 4-16 (bottom left)

Visual Thinking
Look for a pattern. Draw the fourth figure to complete the pattern.

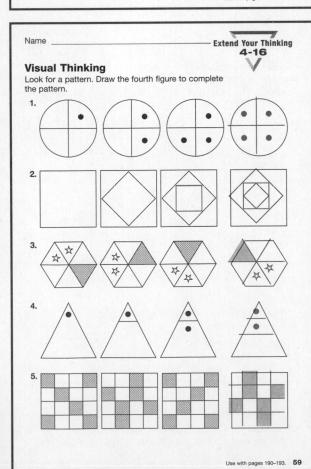

1.

2.

3.

4.

5.

Worksheet 5-1 (bottom right)

Visual Thinking
Continue the pattern. Draw the next two sets of beads.

1.

2.

3.

4.

5.

6.

7.

For 7, look at both rows.

Name _____

Decision Making
You can make warm fleece scarves to sell!

Here's how:

1. 2 feet of fleece fabric makes 3 scarves.
2. Cut the fabric into 3 strips. Each strip will be 6 inches wide.
3. To make a fringe, cut notches on each end. Tie knots in some of the pieces of fringe.

|← 2 ft →|
6 inches
6 inches
6 inches

You can buy 2 feet of fabric for $6. You can sell each scarf for any price you wish.

1. a. How many scarves can you make with 2 feet of fabric?
   __3 scarves__

   b. How much does 2 feet of fabric cost? __$6__

   c. Suppose you sell 1 scarf for $5. How much will you get for 3 scarves? 3 × $5 = __$15__

   d. How much money will you make from 3 scarves?
   __$15__ – $6 = __$9__

2. a. How many scarves will you make? _____
   b. How much fabric will you buy? _____
   c. What will be the price of each scarf? _____
   d. How much money will you make? $_____

   Check students' answers. The answer for b.
   should be the answer for a. × 2 divided by 3.
   The answer for d. should be (c. × a.) – ($2 × a.)

Use with pages 206–207. **61**

Name _____

Patterns in Numbers
Complete the pattern.

1. 2, 4, __6__, 8, 10, __12__, 14
2. 3, 6, 9, __12__, __15__, 18
3. 1, 5, 9, __13__, __17__, __21__
4. __5__, 10, 15, 20, __25__, 30
5. 4, 12, 20, 28, __36__, __44__
6. __10__, __20__, 30, 40, 50, 60
7. 4, __8__, 12, 16, 20, __24__

Make up your own number patterns. Leave two blank spaces. Give them to a classmate to solve. **Answers will vary.**

8. ___, ___, ___, ___, ___, ___
9. ___, ___, ___, ___, ___, ___
10. ___, ___, ___, ___, ___, ___

11. On Sunday night Sylvie had 10 pennies in a jar. If she put 2 more pennies in each morning, how many pennies would she have on Friday night? Skip count on a calendar to find the answer.
    __20__

12. When do you use number patterns? Think about number patterns in math or other subjects. Think about number patterns at home. Give as many examples as you can.
    Possible answers: I use number patterns to skip-count and
    multiply. I count by 5s to tell time. I count things like pennies
    by 2s or 5s.

62 Use with pages 208–209.

Name _____

Visual Thinking
Ring the figures in each row that are the same.

1.

2.

3.

4.

5.

6.

Use with pages 212–213. **63**

Name _____

Patterns in Algebra
Complete.

1. a. 2 × __1__ = 2
   b. 2 × __2__ = 4
   c. 2 × __3__ = 6
   d. 2 × __4__ = 8

2. a. 5 × __2__ = 10
   b. 5 × __3__ = 15
   c. 5 × __4__ = 20
   d. 5 × __5__ = 25

3. a. 5 × __4__ = 20
   b. 5 × __5__ = 25
   c. 5 × __6__ = 30
   d. 5 × __7__ = 35

4. a. 2 × __6__ = 12
   b. 2 × __7__ = 14
   c. 2 × __8__ = 16
   d. 2 × __9__ = 18

5. a. 5 × __8__ = 40
   b. 5 × __9__ = 45
   c. 5 × __10__ = 50
   d. 5 × __11__ = 55

6. a. 2 × __9__ = 18
   b. 2 × __10__ = 20
   c. 2 × __11__ = 22
   d. 2 × __12__ = 24

7. a. 5 × __3__ = 15
   b. __5__ × 4 = 20
   c. 5 × 5 = __25__
   d. __5__ × 6 = 30

8. a. 5 × __6__ = 30
   b. __5__ × 7 = 35
   c. 5 × 8 = __40__
   d. __5__ × 9 = 45

9. From above, you know
   5 × 8 = 40 and
   5 × 9 = 45.
   How could you find
   5 × 17?
   Add the products of 5 × 8 and 5 × 9; 5 × 17 = 85

10. How could you find the product of 2 × 19?
    Add the products of 2 × 9 and 2 × 10; 2 × 19 = 38

64 Use with pages 214–215.

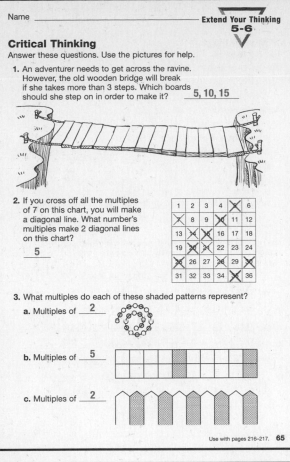

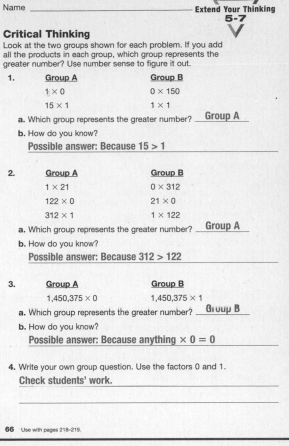

Critical Thinking

Answer these questions. Use the pictures for help.

1. An adventurer needs to get across the ravine. However, the old wooden bridge will break if she takes more than 3 steps. Which boards should she step on in order to make it? **5, 10, 15**

2. If you cross off all the multiples of 7 on this chart, you will make a diagonal line. What number's multiples make 2 diagonal lines on this chart?
   5

1	2	3	4	✗	6
✗	8	9	✗	11	12
13	✗	✗	16	17	18
19	✗	✗	22	23	24
✗	26	27	✗	29	✗
31	32	33	34	✗	36

3. What multiples do each of these shaded patterns represent?
   a. Multiples of __2__

   b. Multiples of __5__

   c. Multiples of __2__

Critical Thinking

Look at the two groups shown for each problem. If you add all the products in each group, which group represents the greater number? Use number sense to figure it out.

1.
Group A	Group B
1×0	0×150
15×1	1×1

   a. Which group represents the greater number? __Group A__

   b. How do you know?
   Possible answer: Because 15 > 1

2.
Group A	Group B
1×21	0×312
122×0	21×0
312×1	1×122

   a. Which group represents the greater number? __Group A__

   b. How do you know?
   Possible answer: Because 312 > 122

3.
Group A	Group B
$1,450,375 \times 0$	$1,450,375 \times 1$

   a. Which group represents the greater number? __Group B__

   b. How do you know?
   Possible answer: Because anything $\times$ 0 = 0

4. Write your own group question. Use the factors 0 and 1.
   Check students' work.

Patterns in Numbers

Write the next three numbers to continue the pattern. Then write the rule used to make the pattern.

1. 6, 8, 10, __12__, __14__, __16__
   Rule: __Add 2, or find next multiple of 2.__

2. 25, 30, 35, __40__, __45__, __50__
   Rule: __Add 5, or find next multiple of 5.__

3. 27, 36, 45, __54__, __63__, __72__
   Rule: __Add 9, or find next multiple of 9.__

4. 7, 10, 13, 16, 19, __22__, __25__, __28__
   Rule: __Add 3.__

5. 80, 85, 90, 95, __100__, __105__, __110__
   Rule: __Add 5.__

6. 5, 6, 8, 11, 15, __20__, __26__, __33__
   Rule: __Add 1, add 2, add 3 and so on.__

7. 96, 92, 88, 84, __80__, __76__, __72__
   Rule: __Subtract 4.__

8. 100, 99, 97, 94, 90, __85__, __79__, __72__
   Rule: __Take away 1, then 2, then 3, then 4, and so on.__

9. 10, 19, 28, 37, 46, __55__, __64__, __73__
   Rule: __Add 9.__

10. 72, 63, 54, 45, __36__, __27__, __18__
    Rule: __Subtract 9.__

11. 18, 36, 54, 72, __90__, __108__, __126__
    Rule: __Add 18.__

Critical Thinking

The Mississippi River is often called the "Mighty Mississippi." However, without the help of the Missouri and Ohio Rivers, the Mississippi wouldn't amount to all that much.

The Mississippi is an average-sized river that flows out of Lake Itasca in Minnesota. But it gets bigger near St. Louis, where the Missouri joins it after a 2,466-mile journey. Then the Ohio links up at Cairo, Illinois, after its journey of 980 miles.

By the time the Mississippi finishes its own journey and empties into the Gulf of Mexico, it's one of the longest and most powerful rivers in the world.

1. What kind of information do you know from this article?
   Possible answer: What rivers join the Mississippi, where they join, how long they are

2. What information would you like to know that isn't given in the article?
   Possible answer: How long the Mississippi is

3. Can you find the difference in length between the Mississippi and Missouri rivers? If so, write a number sentence here that shows it.
   No; Not enough information

4. Can you find the difference in length between the Missouri and Ohio rivers? If so, write a number sentence here that shows it.
   Yes; 2,466 − 980 = 1,486

5. Would you say that the Mississippi is longer or shorter than the Missouri river? What makes you think so?
   Possible answer: The Mississippi may be longer because it is described as one of the longest rivers in the world.

Critical Thinking

Decide which operation will help you solve each problem.
Then explain how you would solve the problem.

1. You are making invitations for a big family dinner party. Before you send them, your mother decides to invite more people. You need to figure out how many invitations to make.

   __Add the number of new guests to the total number.__

2. You are baking a cake for the party. The recipe makes enough batter for a one-layer cake. You would like to make a two-layer cake. You need to know how much more of each ingredient to use.

   __Multiply each ingredient by 2.__

3. You are making snacks for the party. Your father suggests that you make at least 5 snacks for each guest. You need to know how many snacks to make.

   __Multiply the number of guests by 5.__

4. Your family is serving chicken pot-pies at the party. Each guest gets his or her own pie. At the last minute, some guests call to say they won't be coming. You need to know how many pot-pies to bake.

   __Subtract the number of guests who aren't coming from the__
   __total number of guests.__

5. You are setting the table for the dinner party. Every place setting will have two drinking glasses. You need to know how many drinking glasses to take from the cupboard.

   __Multiply the number of places by 2.__

6. Before you relax and enjoy the party you need to make the fruit drink. Each guest will drink 2 cups. You need to know how many cups to make.

   __Multiply the number of guests by 2.__

Critical Thinking

There are 16 groups of 3 in 48. $16 \times 3 = $ **48**
There are 24 groups of 3 in 72. $24 \times 3 = $ **72**
There are 41 groups of 3 in 123. $41 \times 3 = $ **123**

Add the digits in each product above.

1. What is the sum of $4 + 8$? __12__
2. What is the sum of $7 + 2$? __9__
3. What is the sum of $1 + 2 + 3$? __6__
4. Describe the patterns you see. __Possible answer: Each sum is a__ __multiple of 3.__
5. How could you use this information to determine if a number contains an equal number of groups of three?
   __Add the digits that make up the number. If they total to a__
   __multiple of 3, they contain an equal number of groups of 3.__

Use the pattern to predict whether each number contains an equal number of groups of three. Explain how you made your prediction.

6. 45   __Yes; $4 + 5 = 9$, 9 is the product of 3×3.__
7. 78   __Yes; $7 + 8 = 15$, 15 is the product of 3×5.__
8. 103   __No; $1 + 0 + 3 = 4$, 4 is not a multiple of 3.__
9. 162   __Yes; $1 + 6 + 2 = 9$, 9 is the product of 3×3.__
10. 222   __Yes; $2 + 2 + 2 = 6$, 6 is the product of 3×2.__
11. 263   __No; $2 + 6 + 3 = 11$, 11 is not a multiple of 3.__
12. 147   __Yes; $1 + 4 + 7 = 12$, 12 is the product of 3×4.__
13. 352   __No; $3 + 5 + 2 = 10$, 10 is not a multiple of 3.__

Visual Thinking

1. These figures are all woggles. How are woggles alike?

   __All contain two of the same figure in varying sizes.__

2. Circle the woggle.

3. These figures are all tripsoms. How are tripsoms alike?

   __All contain 3 connected, similar figures.__

4. Circle the tripsom.

Patterns in Algebra

Complete the table. Write the rule.

1.
In	9	2	5	7	4	0	8
Out	27	6	15	21	12	0	24

Rule: __Multiply by 3.__

2.
In	10	4	8	9	5	1	7
Out	20	8	16	18	10	2	14

Rule: __Multiply by 2.__

3.
In	3	5	7	9	8	6	4
Out	15	25	35	45	40	30	20

Rule: __Multiply by 5.__

4.
In	3	1	7	0	6	4	2
Out	27	9	63	0	54	36	18

Rule: __Multiply by 9.__

5.
In	9	4	7	5	8	1	6
Out	36	16	28	20	32	4	24

Rule: __Multiply by 4.__

6.
In	7	2	6	3	0	5
Out	42	12	36	18	0	30

Rule: __Multiply by 6.__

Critical Thinking

Extend Your Thinking 6-4

Mark must read a book for a book report. He has chosen a book about Mickey Mantle. Mark has made a reading plan. He will read 7 pages one day, 8 pages the next and continue this plan.

1. On what day will Mark start reading Chapter 2?

Day 3

TABLE OF CONTENTS
Chapter 1 1
Chapter 2 26
Chapter 3 40
Chapter 4 52
Chapter 5 64
Chapter 6 76
Chapter 7 90

2. How many pages will Mark have read after 4 days?

30 pages

3. What chapter will Mark be on after reading for 8 days? How do you know?

Chapter 5; Possible answer: 7 × 4 = 28, 8 × 4 = 32,

28 + 32 = 60, Chapter 5 has pages 52 to 64.

4. On what day will Mark start reading Chapter 8? How do you know? Explain.

Day 12; Possible answer: Mark is on page 60 on Day 8. He

has 30 more pages until Chapter 8. 7 × 2 = 14, 8 × 2 = 16;

14 + 16 + 60 = 90

5. The book has 120 pages. Describe how you can find out how long it will take Mark to finish the book. How many days will Mark need to finish the book?

Possible answer: Guess and check until you

find the correct answer; 16 days

Use with pages 246–247. **73**

Patterns in Numbers

Extend Your Thinking 6-5

Tell what rule was used to make the pattern. What are the next three numbers?

1. 2, 4, 6, 8, __10__, __12__, __14__
Rule: **Add 2.**

2. 5, 10, 15, 20, __25__, __30__, __35__
Rule: **Add 5.**

3. 3, 6, 9, 12, __15__, __18__, __21__
Rule: **Add 3.**

4. 6, 12, 18, 24, __30__, __36__, __42__
Rule: **Add 6.**

5. 4, 8, 12, 16, __20__, __24__, __28__
Rule: **Add 4.**

6. 7, 14, 21, 28, __35__, __42__, __49__
Rule: **Add 7.**

7. What patterns do you find in **1–6**? Explain.

Possible answer: The first number is multiplied by 2 to get the

2nd number, multiplied by 3 to get the 3rd number, and so on.

8. In the pattern that begins 8, 16, 24 . . . what would the 6th number be?   **48**

9. In the pattern that begins 9, 18, 27 . . . what would the 5th number be?   **45**

74 Use with pages 250–251.

Patterns in Numbers

Extend Your Thinking 6-6

1	2	3	4	5	6	7	8	9	10
11	12	13	14	15	16	17	18	19	20
21	22	23	24	25	26	27	28	29	30
31	32	33	34	35	36	37	38	39	40
41	42	43	44	45	46	47	48	49	50
51	52	53	54	55	56	57	58	59	60
61	62	63	64	65	66	67	68	69	70
71	72	73	74	75	76	77	78	79	80
81	82	83	84	85	86	87	88	89	90
91	92	93	94	95	96	97	98	99	100

Fill in the blanks with the correct numbers. Use the hundred chart above to help you find the patterns.

1. 3, 6, __9__, 12, __15__, __18__

2. 6, __12__, 18, __24__, 30, __36__

3. __24__, 27, 30, __33__, __36__, 39

4. 36, __42__, __48__, 54, __60__, 66

5. __51__, 54, 57, __60__, 63, __66__

6. 66, 72, __78__, __84__, __90__, 96

7. __36__, 39, __42__, 45, __48__, 51

8. 21, __18__, 15, 12, __9__, __6__

9. 42, 36, __30__, __24__, 18, __12__

10. __96__, 93, __90__, __87__, 84, 81

Use with pages 254–255. **75**

Patterns in Multiplication

Extend Your Thinking 6-7

×	0	1	2	3	4	5	6	7	8	9	10	11	12
0	0	0	0	0	0	0	0	0	0	0	0	0	0
1	0	1	2	3	4	5	6	7	8	9	10	11	12
2	0	2	4	6	8	10	12	14	16	18	20	22	24
3	0	3	6	9	12	15	18	21	24	27	30	33	36
4	0	4	8	12	16	20	24	28	32	36	40	44	48
5	0	5	10	15	20	25	30	35	40	45	50	55	60
6	0	6	12	18	24	30	36	42	48	54	60	66	72
7	0	7	14	21	28	35	42	49	56	63	70	77	84
8	0	8	16	24	32	40	48	56	64	72	80	88	96
9	0	9	18	27	36	45	54	63	72	81	90	99	108
10	0	10	20	30	40	50	60	70	80	90	100	110	120
11	0	11	22	33	44	55	66	77	88	99	110	121	132
12	0	12	24	36	48	60	72	84	96	108	120	132	144

Continue each pattern. Use the fact table to help.

1. 7, 14, 21, __28__, __35__, __42__

2. 16, 24, 32, __40__, __48__, __56__

3. 48, 42, 36, __30__, __24__, __18__

4. 27, 36, 45, __54__, __63__, __72__

5. 80, 90, 100, __110__, __120__, __130__

6. 144, 132, 120, __108__, __96__, __84__

7. 121, 100, 81, __64__, __49__, __36__

8. 90, 81, 72, __63__, __54__, __45__

9. 2, 6, 12, __20__, __30__, __42__

10. 0, 1, 4, 9, __16__, __25__, __36__

11. 36, 44, 50, 54, __56__, __56__, __54__

12. 9, 18, 27, __36__, __45__, 54, __63__, 70

76 Use with pages 256–257.

Quadrant 1 (top-left)

Name _____

Critical Thinking

Your family is going away for 5 days. You are leaving early on Saturday morning. Your neighbor, Mr. Pitt, has agreed to come in at noon each day to feed your two cats while you are away. Each cat needs 3 scoops of dry food each day.

1. How many scoops of food will the cats have been fed after 3 days?

   a. Write the number sentence that will help you solve the problem.
   $3 \times 2 \times 3$

   b. What is the answer? __18 scoops__

2. How many scoops of food will Mr. Pitt have fed the cats by the end of the day on Wednesday?

   a. Write the number sentence that will help you solve the problem.
   $3 \times 2 \times 5$

   b. What is the answer? __30 scoops__

3. Suppose you also have 3 dogs that eat 5 scoops of dry food each daily. Describe how you can find out how many scoops of food your pets will be fed while you are away.

   $5 \times 3 \times 5 = 25 \times 3$; Count 3 groups of 25; $25 \times 3 = 75$.

   75 scoops of food for the dogs and 30 scoops for the cats;

   $75 + 30 = 105$ scoops

4. Your friend Alan's family is also going away for 5 days. They have 2 dogs who each eat 4 scoops of food every day. How many scoops will the dogs need to be fed while Alan's family is away?

   40 scoops

Quadrant 2 (top-right)

Name _____

Decision Making

You are planning a lunch party. There will be 35 people. Three different restaurants can serve the guests at your party. You need to decide which restaurant to hire.

A. **Manny's Restaurant**

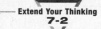
Menu
3 dozen chicken sandwiches
8 six-packs of lemonade
40 oranges
Total cost: $210

B. **Jill's Cafe**

Menu
40 ham and cheese sandwiches
7 six-packs of juice
35 bags of peanuts
Total cost: $234

C. **Doug's Diner**

Menu
38 turkey sandwiches
42 cans of lemonade
3 dozen apples
Total cost: $228

1. Order the choices from most expensive to least expensive.

   B–Jill's Cafe

   C–Doug's Diner

   A–Manny's Restaurant

2. Order the choices from greatest number of food items to least number of food items.

   A–Manny's Restaurant

   B–Jill's Cafe

   C–Doug's Diner

3. If each guest only has one sandwich, one bag of peanuts or piece of fruit, and one drink, how many leftovers will there be for each restaurant choice?

   A. 1 sandwich, 13 lemonades, 5 oranges

   B. 5 sandwiches, 7 juice cans

   C. 3 sandwiches, 7 lemonades, 1 apple

4. Which restaurant would you hire? Why?

   Possible answer: Jill's Cafe; because my friends prefer juice to lemonade, and there will be extra sandwiches if people are hungry.

Quadrant 3 (bottom-left)

Name _____

Visual Thinking

1. Draw six pieces of pepperoni on the pizza so that each slice gets the same number of pieces of pepperoni.

   How many are on each slice? __2__

2. Draw twelve pieces of pepperoni on the pizza so that each slice gets the same number of pieces of pepperoni.

   How many are on each slice? __3__

3. Draw twelve pieces of pepperoni on the pizza so that each slice gets the same number of pieces of pepperoni.

   How many are on each slice? __2__

4. Draw fifteen pieces of pepperoni on the pizza so that each slice gets the same number of pieces of pepperoni.

   How many are on each slice? __5__

Quadrant 4 (bottom-right)

Name _____

Decision Making

A nature club is planning an overnight camping trip. There will be 24 campers. They need to decide how many tents to bring on their trip. Not all of the tents will shelter the same number of sleepers. Here is a list of the different tent sizes.

This is the large tent. It will sleep 6 people.

This is the medium tent. It will sleep 4 people.

This is the small tent. It will sleep 2 people.

1. If the campers decide to bring only large tents, how many tents will they need to bring? __4 tents__

2. If they decide to bring only medium tents, how many will they need to bring? __6 tents__

3. If they decide to bring only small tents, how many will they need to bring? __12 tents__

4. What other combinations of tents could they bring so that there is exactly enough room for everyone to sleep?

   Possible answer: They could bring 2 tents that sleep 6, 2 tents that sleep 4, and 2 tents that sleep 2.

5. Which tents do you think the club should take? Explain your reasoning.

   Possible answers: Bring only the large tents so there is less to carry. Bring only the small tents because they should be lighter and easier to carry for one person.

Critical Thinking

Lisa and 7 of her friends went apple picking. They picked several different kinds of apples. After they were finished picking, they put all of their apples together and counted what they had. They had 24 Macintosh apples, 48 Red Delicious apples, 16 Empire apples, and 8 Cortland apples. They decided that they should share all of the apples equally. Below are 8 bags, one for each person. Decide how many of each kind of apple each person should get, then draw the apples in the bags. Use the letters "M" for Macintosh, "R" for Red Delicious, "E" for Empire, and "C" for Cortland.

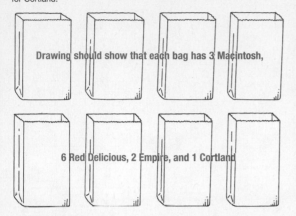

Drawing should show that each bag has 3 Macintosh,

6 Red Delicious, 2 Empire, and 1 Cortland

How did you decide how many of each type of apple to put in each bag?

Possible answer: Drew 1 of each apple in each bag until they were all gone.

Patterns in Numbers

Write the next number in each pattern. Use your knowledge of multiplication facts.

1. 15, 18, 21, 24, __27__
2. 6, 12, 18, 24, __30__
3. 21, 28, 35, 42, __49__
4. 45, 40, 35, 30, __25__
5. 48, 40, 32, 24, __16__

Fill in the missing number using your knowledge of multiplication facts.

6. 16, 20, 24, __28__, 32
7. 8, 10, __12__, 14, 16
8. 9, __12__, 15, 18, 21
9. 49, 42, 35, __28__, 21
10. __48__, 40, 32, 24, 16

Divide by 2. Then divide the result by 2. Keep dividing by 2 until you cannot go any further.

11. 16
$$16 \div 2 = 8, 8 \div 2 = 4, 4 \div 2 = 2, 2 \div 2 = 1$$

Divide by 0. Then divide the result by 3. Keep dividing by 3 until you cannot go any further.

12. 27
$$27 \div 3 = 9, 9 \div 3 = 3, 3 \div 3 = 1$$

Divide by 4. Then divide the result by 4. Keep dividing by 4 until you cannot go any further.

11. 64
$$64 \div 4 = 16, 16 \div 4 = 4, 4 \div 4 = 1$$

Critical Thinking

1. Find four ways to draw one straight line between the dots so that the dots are divided into equal numbers.

2. Find three ways to cut the cake in half so that each half has three cherries on top.

3. Jacob found 28 fossils on his hike. He gave half to his friend. How many did his friend get? __14 fossils__

4. Mary found 22 rocks on her vacation. She gave half to her sister. How many did Mary keep? __11 rocks__

5. On Monday, Clara and Beth's grandmother gave them 24 pennies to share equally. How much did each person get?
__12 pennies__

6. On Tuesday, Clara and Beth's grandmother gave them 30 pennies to share. How much did each person get?
__15 pennies__

7. What strategy did you use to solve 3–6?
Possible answer: Draw a Picture

8. How could you use place value to solve each problem?
Possible answer: Divide the tens by 2, and divide the ones by 2. Then add the two results.

Critical Thinking

Joe's Market employs 5 workers and pays them each $5 per hour.

1. John makes $30 one day. How many hours did he work? __6 hours__

2. Amy makes $45 over two days. How many hours did she work? __9 hours__

3. Louis earned $35 on Tuesday and $25 on Thursday. How many hours did he work all together?
__12 hours__

4. If John worked for 5 hours, how much money did he make? __$25__

5. Omar worked for 8 hours and Jenny worked for 6 hours.
   a. How many more hours did Omar work than Jenny? __2 hours__
   b. How much more money did Omar make than Jenny? __$10__

6. Louis made $15 on Monday, $20 on Tuesday, and $40 on Wednesday.
   a. How many hours did he work on each day?
   __Monday–3 hours, Tuesday–4 hours, Wednesday–8 hours__
   b. How much did he earn over the three days? __$75__
   c. How much would he have earned if he had worked twice as long on Monday and half as long on Wednesday? __$70__

Patterns in Numbers
Fill in the blanks to complete the patterns.

1. 3, 6, 9, __12__, __15__, __18__
2. 12, 16, 20, __24__, __28__, __32__
3. 20, 25, 30, __35__, __40__, __45__
4. 27, 24, 21, __18__, __15__, __12__
5. 35, 30, 25, __20__, __15__, __10__
6. 36, 32, 28, __24__, __20__, __16__
7. 4, 8, __12__, 16, __20__, __24__
8. 6, __9__, __12__, 15, 18, __21__
9. 5, __10__, 15, __20__, __25__, 30
10. 28, 24, __20__, __16__, 12, __8__
11. 21, __18__, 15, 12, __9__, __6__
12. 45, __40__, __35__, 30, 25, __20__
13. 10, __15__, 20, __25__, 30, __35__
14. 32, __28__, 24, __20__, __16__, 12

15. A teacher divides 32 friendship bracelets among 8 students.
   a. How many does each student get? ____4____
   b. If the students all wear an equal number of friendship bracelets on each wrist, how many does each wear on each wrist? ____2____

16. Shannon has 18 fruit bars. She gives an equal number to each of 3 friends.
   a. How many fruit bars does each student get? __6 fruit bars__
   b. If each friend eats 2 fruit bars a day, how many days will the fruit bars last? __3 days__

Visual Thinking
The counters on the left are to be placed in the boxes on the right so that there are an equal number of counters in each box. Circle the correct answer from the choices on the right. Follow the example.

Example:

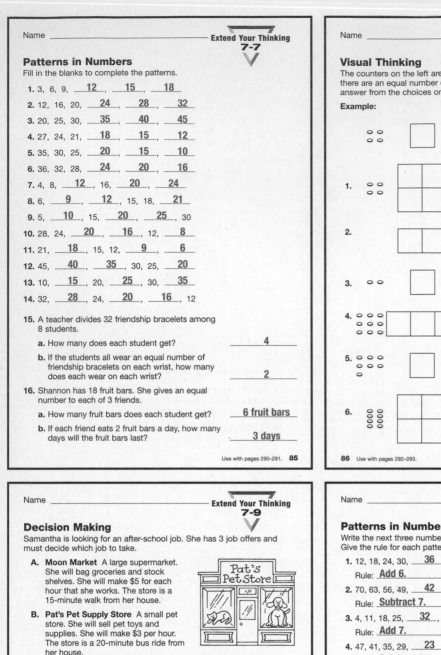

Decision Making
Samantha is looking for an after-school job. She has 3 job offers and must decide which job to take.

A. **Moon Market** A large supermarket. She will bag groceries and stock shelves. She will make $5 for each hour that she works. The store is a 15-minute walk from her house.

B. **Pat's Pet Supply Store** A small pet store. She will sell pet toys and supplies. She will make $3 per hour. The store is a 20-minute bus ride from her house.

C. **Uncle Paul's Corner Store** A very small grocery store. Samantha will work the cash register and bag groceries and stock shelves. She will make $4 per hour. The store is a 2-minute walk from her house.

1. If Samantha works 8 hours each week, how much will she earn at each job?

   Job A: __$40__   Job B: __$24__   Job C: __$32__

2. Which job would be the most difficult for traveling from Samantha's house? Explain.

   __Possible answer: Pat's Pet Supply Store (Job B); because__
   __Samantha would need to take a 20-minute bus ride__

3. Which job do you think would be the most fun? Explain.

   __Answers will vary.__
   _____

4. Which job offer should Samantha take? Explain your reasoning.

   __Possible answer: She should choose to work at Moon Market__
   __(Job A) because it pays the most money and it is only a__
   __15-minute walk from her house.__

Patterns in Numbers
Write the next three numbers.
Give the rule for each pattern.

1. 12, 18, 24, 30, __36__, __42__, __48__
   Rule: __Add 6.__
2. 70, 63, 56, 49, __42__, __35__, __28__
   Rule: __Subtract 7.__
3. 4, 11, 18, 25, __32__, __39__, __46__
   Rule: __Add 7.__
4. 47, 41, 35, 29, __23__, __17__, __11__
   Rule: __Subtract 6.__
5. 24, 21, 18, 15, __12__, __9__, __6__
   Rule: __Subtract 3.__
6. 1; 4; 16; 64; __256__; __1,024__; __4,096__
   Rule: __Multiply by 4.__
7. 96, 48, 24, __12__, __6__, __3__
   Rule: __Divide by 2.__
8. 3; 33; 333; __3,333__; __33,333__; __333,333__
   Rule: __Add 30; 300; 3,000; 30,000; 300,000__
9. 4, 11, 25, 46, __74__, __109__, __151__
   Rule: __Add 7, 14, 21, 28, 35, 42.__
10. Make up your own patterns. Give each rule.
   __Answers will vary.__
   Rule: _____

   Rule: _____

Critical Thinking

1. Draw lines to divide each set of squares in half. **Possible answers:**

a. What is 8 ÷ 2? **4**

b. What is 8 ÷ 4? **2**

c. Count the total number of squares.
What is 24 ÷ 8? **3**

2. Draw lines to divide the squares into groups of 9.

a. How many squares are there in all? **36**

b. What is the number of squares divided by 9? **4**

3. 45 flowers are divided among 9 people. How many flowers does each person get? **5**

4. The Happy Snack Company is giving away free samples of dried apricots. It gives away 72 apricots to the first 9 people.

a. How many apricots does each person get? **8**

b. The company gives away 56 apricots to the next 8 people. How many apricots does each person get? **7**

5. I have $54. I buy 9 equally priced gifts. How much does each one cost? **$6**

Critical Thinking

Here are two 50 square grids. The first lists the even numbers from 2 to 50. The second lists the odd numbers from 1 to 49. Some numbers are missing.

Fill in the missing numbers.

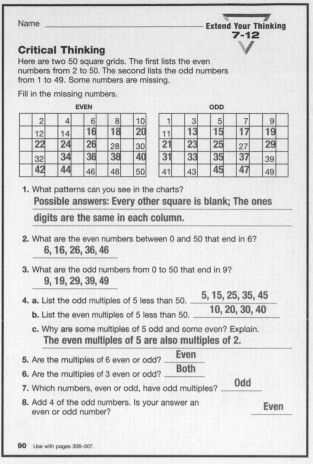

EVEN

2	4	6	8	10
12	14	16	18	20
22	24	26	28	30
32	34	36	38	40
42	44	46	48	50

ODD

1	3	5	7	9
11	13	15	17	19
21	23	25	27	29
31	33	35	37	39
41	43	45	47	49

1. What patterns can you see in the charts?
Possible answers: Every other square is blank; The ones digits are the same in each column.

2. What are the even numbers between 0 and 50 that end in 6?
6, 16, 26, 36, 46

3. What are the odd numbers from 0 to 50 that end in 9?
9, 19, 29, 39, 49

4. a. List the odd multiples of 5 less than 50. **5, 15, 25, 35, 45**

b. List the even multiples of 5 less than 50. **10, 20, 30, 40**

c. Why are some multiples of 5 odd and some even? Explain.
The even multiples of 5 are also multiples of 2.

5. Are the multiples of 6 even or odd? **Even**

6. Are the multiples of 3 even or odd? **Both**

7. Which numbers, even or odd, have odd multiples? **Odd**

8. Add 4 of the odd numbers. Is your answer an even or odd number? **Even**

Decision Making

The reading club at school is having a pizza party. They can afford two large pizzas with 2 toppings but they cannot decide on the toppings. Charles wants to draw a picture and Linda wants to make a list to display all the choices so the club can make a decision. They try both ways.

These toppings are available: sausage, black olives, ham, onions, and green pepper.

Charles' picture

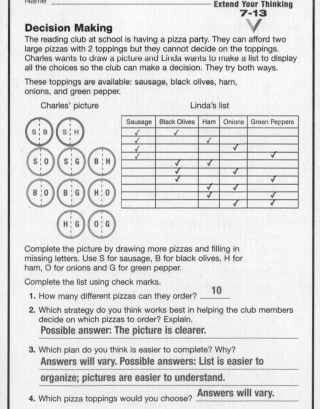

Linda's list

Sausage	Black Olives	Ham	Onions	Green Peppers
✓	✓			
✓		✓		
✓			✓	
✓				✓
	✓	✓		
	✓		✓	
	✓			✓
		✓	✓	
		✓		✓
			✓	✓

Complete the picture by drawing more pizzas and filling in missing letters. Use S for sausage, B for black olives, H for ham, O for onions and G for green pepper.

Complete the list using check marks.

1. How many different pizzas can they order? **10**

2. Which strategy do you think works best in helping the club members decide on which pizzas to order? Explain.
Possible answer: The picture is clearer.

3. Which plan do you think is easier to complete? Why?
Answers will vary. Possible answers: List is easier to organize; pictures are easier to understand.

4. Which pizza toppings would you choose? **Answers will vary.**

Visual Thinking

Draw the shape or shapes that balance each scale.

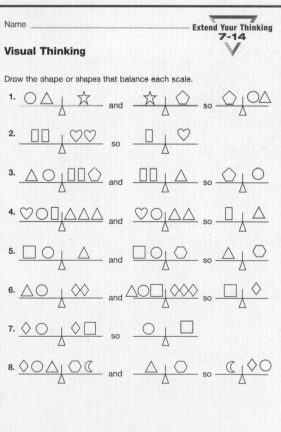

1.

2.

3.

4.

5.

6.

7.

8.

177

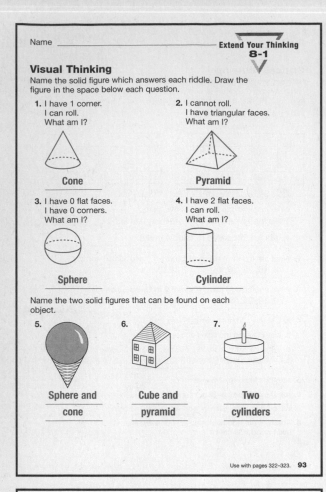

Extend Your Thinking
8-1

Visual Thinking

Name the solid figure which answers each riddle. Draw the figure in the space below each question.

1. I have 1 corner.
I can roll.
What am I?

Cone

2. I cannot roll.
I have triangular faces.
What am I?

Pyramid

3. I have 0 flat faces.
I have 0 corners.
What am I?

Sphere

4. I have 2 flat faces.
I can roll.
What am I?

Cylinder

Name the two solid figures that can be found on each object.

5.

Sphere and

cone

6.

Cube and

pyramid

7.

Two

cylinders

Use with pages 322–323. **93**

Extend Your Thinking
8-2

Visual Thinking

What comes next in the pattern? Draw the shape.

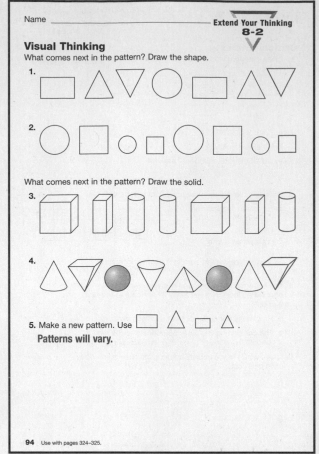

1.

2.

What comes next in the pattern? Draw the solid.

3.

4.

5. Make a new pattern. Use ▭ △ ▭ △ .
Patterns will vary.

94 Use with pages 324–325.

Extend Your Thinking
8-3

Critical Thinking

Look at the drawing. Use it to answer the questions.

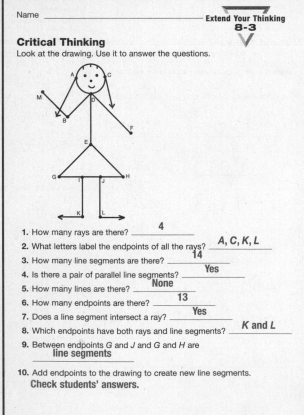

1. How many rays are there? _____ **4**

2. What letters label the endpoints of all the rays? **A, C, K, L**

3. How many line segments are there? _____ **14**

4. Is there a pair of parallel line segments? _____ **Yes**

5. How many lines are there? _____ **None**

6. How many endpoints are there? _____ **13**

7. Does a line segment intersect a ray? _____ **Yes**

8. Which endpoints have both rays and line segments? **K and L**

9. Between endpoints G and J and G and H are **line segments**

10. Add endpoints to the drawing to create new line segments.
Check students' answers.

Use with pages 326–327. **95**

Extend Your Thinking
8-4

Decision Making

The art club is making a decorative table top. They will paste tiles on a rectangular wooden table top. They must choose one of these three types of tiles to decorate the table.

Type A   Type B   Type C

1. How many right angles does each tile have?
Type A ___**4**___ Type B ___**1**___ Type C ___**0**___

2. How many angles less than a right angle does each tile have?
Type A ___**0**___ Type B ___**2**___ Type C ___**2**___

3. How many angles greater than a right angle does each tile have?
Type A ___**0**___ Type B ___**0**___ Type C ___**2**___

4. Which of the tiles would not fit in the corner of the rectangular table top? Why not?
C; Because there are no right angles in this tile and the corner of the table is a right angle

5. Think about the work needed to fit each type of tile onto the table top. Which tile would you choose for decorating the table? Why?
Type A; Because it is the same shape as the table and will be easiest to fit together on the table top

6. If you wanted to use a greater number of tiles, which would you choose? Why?
Type B; Because we would need twice as many

96 Use with pages 328–329.

Panel 1 (8-5)

Name _____

Extend Your Thinking
8-5

Patterns in Geometry

Find the pattern in each row by identifying each flip, slide, or turn. Circle the move that comes next.

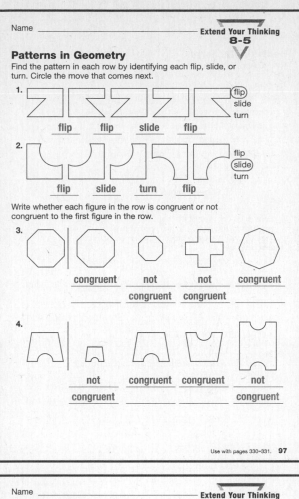

1. flip
    (flip)
    slide
    turn

    flip   flip   slide   flip

2. flip
    (slide)
    turn

    flip   slide   turn   flip

Write whether each figure in the row is congruent or not congruent to the first figure in the row.

3. congruent   not congruent   not congruent   congruent

4. not congruent   congruent   congruent   not congruent

Use with pages 330–331.   **97**

Panel 2 (8-6)

Name _____

Extend Your Thinking
8-6

Critical Thinking

1. Write the numbers 0 through 9.

   Which of these numbers have no lines of symmetry? Explain.
   2, 4, 5, 6, 7, 9; Because if you fold them in half, the parts do not match

2. Which of these numbers have only one line of symmetry? ___3___
   Draw each number with the line of symmetry in the space below.

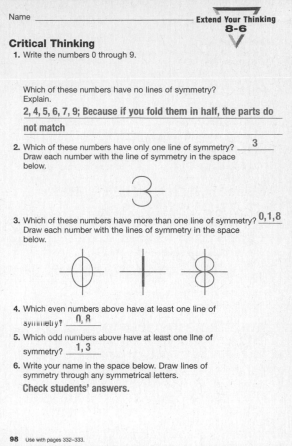

3. Which of these numbers have more than one line of symmetry? 0, 1, 8
   Draw each number with the lines of symmetry in the space below.

4. Which even numbers above have at least one line of symmetry? _0, 8_

5. Which odd numbers above have at least one line of symmetry? _1, 3_

6. Write your name in the space below. Draw lines of symmetry through any symmetrical letters.
   Check students' answers.

98   Use with pages 332–333.

Panel 3 (8-7)

Name _____

Extend Your Thinking
8-7

Patterns in Geometry

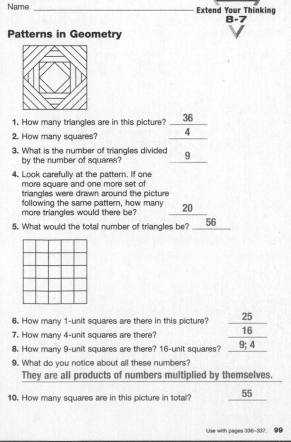

1. How many triangles are in this picture? __36__
2. How many squares? __4__
3. What is the number of triangles divided by the number of squares? __9__
4. Look carefully at the pattern. If one more square and one more set of triangles were drawn around the picture following the same pattern, how many more triangles would there be? __20__
5. What would the total number of triangles be? __56__

6. How many 1-unit squares are there in this picture? __25__
7. How many 4-unit squares are there? __16__
8. How many 9-unit squares are there? 16-unit squares? __9; 4__
9. What do you notice about all these numbers?
   They are all products of numbers multiplied by themselves.

10. How many squares are in this picture in total? __55__

Use with pages 336–337.   **99**

Panel 4 (8-8)

Name _____

Extend Your Thinking
8-8

Patterns in Geometry

Study the perimeters of these shapes. Ring the shape that doesn't belong in the group.

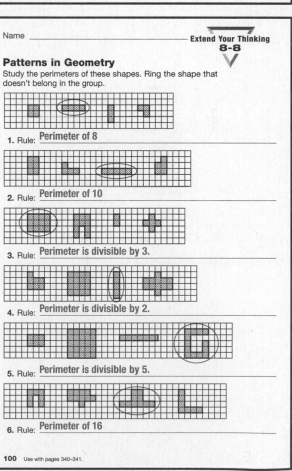

1. Rule: **Perimeter of 8**

2. Rule: **Perimeter of 10**

3. Rule: **Perimeter is divisible by 3.**

4. Rule: **Perimeter is divisible by 2.**

5. Rule: **Perimeter is divisible by 5.**

6. Rule: **Perimeter of 16**

100   Use with pages 340–341.

179

Critical Thinking

Name _____

Extend Your Thinking
8-9

1. What are the areas of the five rectangles inside the square grid?
6, 6, 6, 6, and 12 square units

2. What is the area of the large square grid?
100 square units

3. If you color each rectangle red, how many unit squares will be red? Explain how you found you answer. **36; Possible answer: Add the areas of all the rectangles.**

4. If you color the rest of the grid blue, how many unit squares will be blue? Explain your answer.
Possible answer: 64; Subtract 36 from the total area.

5. What plan would help find the area of this shape without counting each unit square? **Possible answer: Divide the shape into rectangles.**

6. Draw lines to divide the shape. How many smaller rectangles do you have?
Check students' drawings. Possible answer: 5

7. What are the areas of the rectangles?
Possible answers: 4, 8, 12, 16, and 20 square units

8. Explain how you found the areas of the rectangles.
Possible answers: Counted squares or multiplied length by width

9. What is the total area of the shape? Explain how you found the answer.
60 square units; Possible answer: Found the sum of all the pieces

Use with pages 342–343. **101**

Decision Making

Name _____

Extend Your Thinking
8-10

The Science Club is having their winter pizza party. They are going to order thick-crust pan pizza for the dozen members. The pizza comes in three sizes, all rectangular.

A small pizza is 5 inches by 10 inches and costs $4.00.

A medium pizza is 6 inches by 12 inches and costs $6.00.

A large pizza is 10 inches by 15 inches and costs $11.00.

1. Draw arrays on grid paper to show the three sizes of pizza.
Have one square on the grid paper equal one inch.
Find the area of each size of pizza.
Small **50 square inches** Medium **72 square inches**
Large **150 square inches**

2. The last time the club ordered pizza they ordered one large pizza but they didn't have enough. Some members say they should order two large pizzas this time. Some members suggest they order small or medium pizzas and save money.
What should the club members consider when placing their order this time?
Possible answers: They should consider the areas of each size of pizza, the cost of each size, and the fact that they need more than 1 large pizza; they should also calculate the cost of other combinations of pizza.

3. The club estimates that they could have eaten about 250 square inches of pizza last time. What would you suggest? Explain your decision.
Possible answers: They could order 2 large pizzas for $22 and have 50 square inches left over. They could order 1 of each size for $21 and have only 22 square inches left over.

102 Use with pages 344–345.

Visual Thinking

Name _____

Extend Your Thinking
8-11

A face is one side of a figure. A cube has 6 faces.

Use cubes to build this shape. Then answer each question.

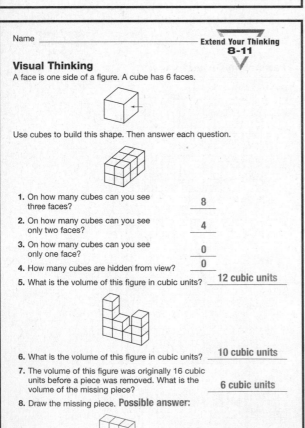

1. On how many cubes can you see three faces? **8**

2. On how many cubes can you see only two faces? **4**

3. On how many cubes can you see only one face? **0**

4. How many cubes are hidden from view? **0**

5. What is the volume of this figure in cubic units? **12 cubic units**

6. What is the volume of this figure in cubic units? **10 cubic units**

7. The volume of this figure was originally 16 cubic units before a piece was removed. What is the volume of the missing piece? **6 cubic units**

8. Draw the missing piece. **Possible answer:**

Use with pages 346–347. **103**

Visual Thinking

Name _____

Extend Your Thinking
8-12

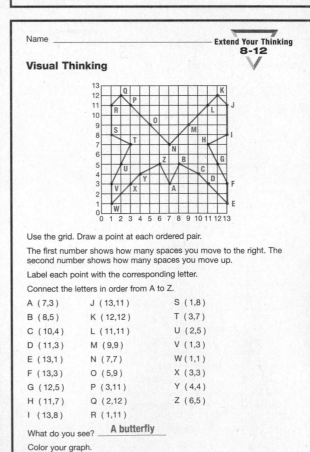

Use the grid. Draw a point at each ordered pair.

The first number shows how many spaces you move to the right. The second number shows how many spaces you move up.

Label each point with the corresponding letter.

Connect the letters in order from A to Z.

A (7,3)   J (13,11)   S (1,8)
B (8,5)   K (12,12)   T (3,7)
C (10,4)   L (11,11)   U (2,5)
D (11,3)   M (9,9)   V (1,3)
E (13,1)   N (7,7)   W (1,1)
F (13,3)   O (5,9)   X (3,3)
G (12,5)   P (3,11)   Y (4,4)
H (11,7)   Q (2,12)   Z (6,5)
I (13,8)   R (1,11)

What do you see? **A butterfly**

Color your graph.

104 Use with pages 348–349.

180

Extend Your Thinking
9-1

Patterns in Numbers

Complete the pattern.

1. 20, 40, __60__, 80, 100, __120__

2. 40, 80, __120__, 160, __200__, 240

3. 90, 180, __270__, 360, __450__, __540__

4. 30, 60, 90, __120__, __150__, 180

5. 70, 140, 210, __280__, __350__, __420__

6. __60__, __120__, 180, 240, 300, __360__

7. __50__, 100, 150, 200, __250__, __300__

8. 80, __160__, 240, 320, __400__, __480__

Make up your own number patterns. Leave two blank spaces
Give them to a classmate to solve.

**Check students' patterns
for a logical progression.**

9. ____, ____, ____, ____, ____, ____

10. ____, ____, ____, ____, ____, ____

11. ____, ____, ____, ____, ____, ____

12. Suppose a number pattern starts with the two numbers **Possible**
shown. Finish the pattern two different ways. **answers shown.**

a. 10, 20, __30__, __40__, __50__

b. 10, 20, __40__, __80__, __160__

Extend Your Thinking
9-2

Critical Thinking

Look at the product. Then write the number that would be
multiplied by 10 to get that product.

1. 210 __21__   2. 300 __30__

3. 240 __24__   4. 150 __15__

5. 180 __18__   6. 320 __32__

7. 80 __8__   8. 360 __36__

9. 750 __75__   10. 520 __52__

Look at the product. Then write the number that would be
multiplied by 100 to get that product.

11. 3,000 __30__   12. 2,400 __24__

13. 4,200 __42__   14. 500 __5__

15. 1,500 __15__   16. 1,800 __18__

17. 2,000 __20__   18. 4,800 __48__

19. 7,500 __75__   20. 6,400 __64__

Look at the product. Then write two possible factors for that
product. **Possible answers shown.**

21. 210 __3, 70__   22. 3,500 __5, 700__

23. 350 __10, 35__   24. 4,800 __6, 800__

25. 150 __3, 50__   26. 1,800 __3, 600__

27. 2,400 __24, 100__   28. 3,600 __6, 600__

29. 1,600 __2, 800__   30. 3,500 __5, 700__

Extend Your Thinking
9-3

Decision Making

The school is building a parking lot
100 feet by 160 feet.

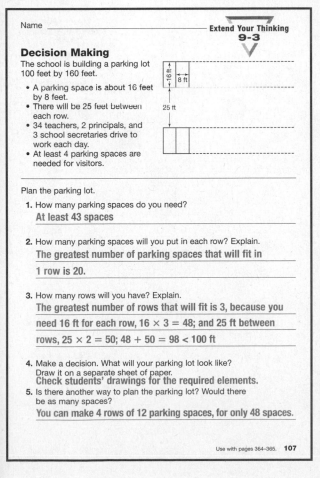

- A parking space is about 16 feet
  by 8 feet.
- There will be 25 feet between
  each row.
- 34 teachers, 2 principals, and
  3 school secretaries drive to
  work each day.
- At least 4 parking spaces are
  needed for visitors.

Plan the parking lot.

1. How many parking spaces do you need?

   At least 43 spaces

2. How many parking spaces will you put in each row? Explain.

   The greatest number of parking spaces that will fit in

   1 row is 20.

3. How many rows will you have? Explain.

   The greatest number of rows that will fit is 3, because you

   need 16 ft for each row, 16 × 3 = 48; and 25 ft between

   rows, 25 × 2 = 50; 48 + 50 = 98 < 100 ft

4. Make a decision. What will your parking lot look like?
   Draw it on a separate sheet of paper.
   Check students' drawings for the required elements.

5. Is there another way to plan the parking lot? Would there
   be as many spaces?
   You can make 4 rows of 12 parking spaces, for only 48 spaces.

Extend Your Thinking
9-4

Visual Thinking

Find the other half of each object below. Draw a line
connecting the two halves.

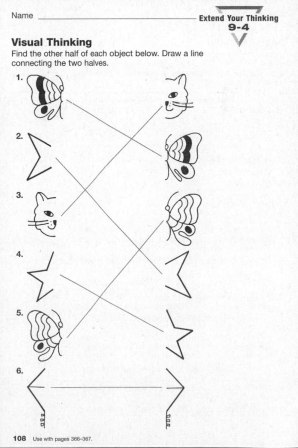

1.

2.

3.

4.

5.

6.

Critical Thinking

Complete each pattern in two different ways. Tell the rule.

1. a. 1, 2, __3__, __4__, __5__

Rule: __Add 1.__

b. 1, 2, __4__, __8__, __16__

Rule: __Multiply by 2.__

2. a. 3, 6, __9__, __12__, __15__

Rule: __Add 3.__

b. 3, 6, __12__, __24__, __48__

Rule: __Multiply by 2.__

3. a. 10, 30, __50__, __70__, __90__

Rule: __Add 20.__

b. 10, 30, __90__, __270__, __810__

Rule: __Multiply by 3.__

4. a. 40, 80, __120__, __160__, __200__

Rule: __Add 40.__

b. 40, 80, __160__, __320__, __640__

Rule: __Multiply by 2.__

Critical Thinking

Suppose you are helping the school secretary with the new book orders. Here is the order list so far:

Title	Boxes Ordered	Books per Box
City Mouse, Country Mouse	8	24
Lyle Goes to the Office	6	36
City Wheels	5	48

1. For which book is the greatest number of copies on order?

City Wheels

2. Suppose 3 boxes of each book arrive. How many more books are still expected? ___324___

3. How many more copies of _Lyle Goes to the Office_ are on order than _City Mouse, Country Mouse_? ___24___

4. Mr. Matlaw, the librarian, wants an equal number of copies of each book for the after-school reading program. What's the least number of boxes he should order of each title?

a. _City Mouse, Country Mouse_: ___6___

b. _Lyle Goes to the Office_: ___4___

c. _City Wheels_: ___3___

d. Describe how you found your answer.

__Possible answer: Multiply each box size (24; 36; 48) by 2,__

__3,4, 5, etc., to see if any of the answers are the same.__

5. Mr. Matlaw wants to order 4 boxes of _Wind in the Willows_. If there are 12 books in each box, how many books will he receive? ___48___

Decision Making

Your club is planning a big trip to visit a distant city. You want to know if your club can afford it. There are 7 members. Your club president made a list of travel costs to 4 of your favorite cities.

From Albuquerque to:	One Round-Trip Ticket Costs:
New York City	$450
Chicago	$480
Los Angeles	$270
Miami	$390

1. How much will it cost the club to go to

a. New York? ___$3,150___

b. Chicago? ___$3,360___

c. Los Angeles? ___$1,890___

d. Miami? ___$2,730___

2. During the last 2 years, your club has raised $2,500. If you vote to use this money towards your trip, which city do you think would be a good choice? Why?

__Possible answer: Los Angeles, because it will cost less__

__than $2,500 for everyone to go__

3. If each club member could raise an additional $100, what other cities would be good choices?

__Possible answer: Miami and New York City__

4. Two club members realize they cannot go on the trip. Will the club's $2,500 be enough for the remaining members to go to Chicago? Explain.

__Yes; 5 × $480 = $2,400; there is enough money.__

5. What additional costs besides airfare should your club consider?

__Possible answers: Lodging, food, museums__

Visual Thinking

Look at each set of figures. Think about how the two images on the left are alike or different. Then, circle the pair of images on the right that have the same relationship.

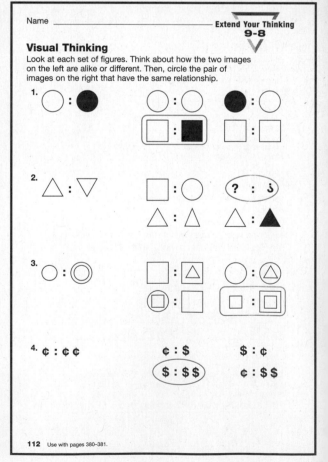

182

Patterns in Data

Extend Your Thinking
9-9

Study the patterns created by the symbols, letters, or numbers. Then, write the next three symbols, letters, or numbers that continue the pattern.

1. Δ, ∞, Δ, ∞, Δ, ∞, Δ, ∞, Δ, ∞, __Δ__ , __∞__ , __Δ__

2. $, $, ¢, ¢, $, $, ¢, ¢, ¢, $ __$__ , __¢__ , __¢__

3. *, *, *, !, *, *, *, !, *, *, *, __!__ , __*__ , __*__

4. +, =, +, +, =, +, +, =, +, __+__ , __=__ , __+__

5. #, #, #, #, ?, #, #, #, ?, #, #, __?__ , __#__ , __?__

6. <, <, >, >, <, >, <, <, >, >, __<__ , __>__ , __<__

7. P, L, S, T, S, L, P, L, S, T, S, __L__ , __P__ , __L__

8. A, A, E, E, I, A, A, E, E, I, A, A, __E__ , __E__ , __I__

9. A, A, E, I, I, O, U, U, A, E, __E__ , __I__ , __O__

10. 2, 4, 5, 7, 8, 10, 11, 13, 14, 16, __17__ , __19__ , __20__

Decision Making

Extend Your Thinking
9-10

The Craft Fair is coming up! Your class has 7 weeks to make 154 pencil holders.

Some weeks, you work faster than others. The class made 20 pencil holders by the end of the first week, 35 by the end of the 2nd week, 55 by the end of the 3rd week, and 70 by the end of the 4th week. There are 3 weeks left.

1. If you let this pattern continue will you have at least 154 pencil holders in 3 more weeks? Explain.

   No; the pattern is 20 + 15 + 20 + 15, etc. At this rate, only 125 pencil holders will be made by the end of 7 weeks.

2. Describe 1 way the class can complete the remaining pencil holders on time.

   Possible answer: Make 28 holders each week for the last 3 weeks.

3. Every other week your class goes to the library and is away from school for a half day. This is why the class didn't make as many pencil holders the 2nd and 4th week. Complete the table. How many pencil holders should the class make each week to meet their goal of 154 pencil holders? **Possible answer shown.**

Week	1	2	3	4	5	6	7
Number made during week	20	15	20	15	30	24	30
Total pencil holders made	20	35	55	70	100	124	154

4. Your class sells the pencil holders for $2 each. How much money would they have made if they had stopped making pencil holders after 4 weeks?

   $140

Critical Thinking

Extend Your Thinking
9-11

The people who live at the River Front Apartments need more parking spaces. They plan to add 14 new rows! They want to assign some of the new rows to each building. Here's what they did.

Building	Spaces Needed	Rows Assigned
Building A	120	4 rows
Building B	60	2 rows
Building C	100	5 rows
Building D	90	3 rows

1. How many cars will Building A need to fit in each row? 30 cars

2. How many cars will Building B need to fit in each row? 30 cars

3. How many cars will Building C need to fit in each row? 20 cars

4. How many cars will Building D need to fit in each row? 30 cars

5. The architect wants all the rows to have the same number of parking spaces. What can she do?

   Possible answer: She could increase the number of spaces in Building C's lot to 120 and make 4 rows with 30 cars in each.

6. How many parking spaces are needed all together?
   370 parking spaces

7. a. Suppose the buildings shared rows. How many rows would they need if each row had 7 parking spaces? 53

   b. Explain how you solved a.
   Possible answer: 350 ÷ 7 = 50, 20 ÷ 7 = 2 R6, so they would need 53 rows of parking in all.

Visual Thinking

Extend Your Thinking
9-12

Look at the shapes on the left in each row. All of the shapes but one are used to make the picture on the right. Circle the shape on the left that is not used.

1.

2.

3.

4.

5.

6.

183

Critical Thinking

You'll need to work backward with quotients and remainders to solve these problems!

Circle the correct answers.

1. Angela gave 6 of her friends each a stick of gum and had 2 left over. How many sticks of gum did she have to start with?

   a. 10 sticks   **b.** 6 sticks   **c.** 8 sticks   **d.** 6 sticks

2. Robert used 13 apples to make 3 apple turnovers. He had 1 apple left over. How many apples did he use in each turnover?

   a. 4 apples   **b.** 3 apples   **c.** 5 apples   **d.** 2 apples

3. San Ho made enough granola to fill 5 tins. Each tin holds 4 pounds. He has 3 pounds left over. How many pounds of granola did San Ho make?

   a. 16 pounds   **b.** 20 pounds   **c.** 14 pounds   **d.** 23 pounds

4. Amir had 48 soup cans to stack on his family's store shelves. 9 cans fit on each shelf. He had 3 cans left over. How many shelves did Amir stack with soup cans?

   a. 3 shelves   **b.** 5 shelves   **c.** 2 shelves   **d.** 6 shelves

5. The Save-the-Earth Club collected enough trash to fill 4 bags. Each bag holds 5 gallons. They have 2 gallons left over. How much trash did they collect?

   a. 22 gallons   **b.** 36 gallons   **c.** 50 gallons   **d.** 31 gallons

6. Each page of Glen's album holds 4 photographs. He filled all 9 pages and still had 3 photos left over. How many photos did Glen have to start with?

   a. 35 photos   **b.** 22 photos   **c.** 25 photos   **d.** 39 photos

7. Kelly gave 4 friends each 4 trading cards and kept 3 for herself. How many cards did she have to start with?

   a. 16 cards   **b.** 11 cards   **c.** 19 cards   **d.** 24 cards

---

Patterns in Numbers

What happens to quotients of the same number when divisors change? Solve these problems and look for patterns.

1. a. $31 \div 4 =$ __7 R3__
   b. $31 \div 5 =$ __6 R1__
   c. $31 \div 6 =$ __5 R1__
   d. $31 \div 7 =$ __4 R3__
   e. $31 \div 8 =$ __3 R7__
   f. $31 \div 9 =$ __3 R4__

2. a. $33 \div 3 =$ __11 R0__
   b. $33 \div 4 =$ __8 R1__
   c. $33 \div 5 =$ __6 R3__
   d. $33 \div 6 =$ __5 R3__
   e. $33 \div 7 =$ __4 R5__
   f. $33 \div 8 =$ __4 R1__

3. a. $47 \div 9 =$ __5 R2__
   b. $47 \div 8 =$ __5 R7__
   c. $47 \div 7 =$ __6 R5__
   d. $47 \div 6 =$ __7 R5__
   e. $47 \div 5 =$ __9 R2__

4. a. $50 \div 9 =$ __5 R5__
   b. $50 \div 8 =$ __6 R2__
   c. $50 \div 7 =$ __7 R1__
   d. $50 \div 6 =$ __8 R2__
   e. $50 \div 5 =$ __10 R0__

5. Describe the patterns that you see.

   Possible answers: As the divisors increase, the quotients decrease. If the quotients stay the same, then the remainders increase or decrease.

Critical Thinking

Your school is having a craft fair in the auditorium. Sellers will rent tables that are 10 feet long. There will be two rows of tables. One row of tables will go against each of the two long walls of the auditorium. These walls are 56 feet long.

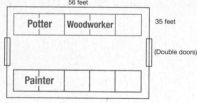

Solve each problem. You may use the picture to help you.

1. How many tables can fit in the auditorium all together? Show how you got your answer. Draw the tables in the diagram above.

   10 tables; Possible answer: 56 ÷ 10 foot tables = 5R6, so 5 tables will fit along each wall. 5 × 2 = 10.

2. 3 people (a potter, a woodworker, and a painter) each want to rent 2 tables. How many tables are left for other people to rent? Label the tables in the diagram above.

   There are 4 tables remaining.

3. If your school wants to raise $500 by renting tables at the fair, how much should people pay per table? Explain how you got your answer.

   Possible answer: $500 ÷ 10 tables = $50 per table.

Visual Thinking

Find the part that completes each shape below. Draw a line connecting the two pieces.

1.
2.
3.
4.
5.
6.

Decision Making

You have been asked to design flags for your school's annual fair. Each grade needs their own flag.

Color the flags according to the instructions.

1. Grade 1 wants $\frac{1}{2}$ of their flag red.

2. Grade 2 wants $\frac{2}{3}$ of their flag green.

3. Grade 3 wants $\frac{3}{4}$ of the circle orange.

4. Grade 4 wants $\frac{3}{8}$ of their flag blue.

5. Grade 5 wants $\frac{1}{2}$ of their flag red and $\frac{1}{4}$ of the flag blue.

6. Grade 6 wants $\frac{1}{2}$ of the middle quadrilateral red and $\frac{1}{2}$ of the rest of the flag green.

Check students' flags for the correct part shaded/colored.

Possible answers given.

Patterns in Numbers

Tell what rule was used to make the pattern. Complete the next three fractions.

1. $\frac{1}{2}, \frac{2}{4}, \frac{3}{6}, \boxed{\frac{4}{8}}, \boxed{\frac{5}{10}}, \boxed{\frac{6}{12}}$

Rule: Possible answer: Make fractions equivalent to $\frac{1}{2}$ by adding 1 to the numerator and 2 to the denominator.

2. $\frac{3}{4}, \frac{6}{8}, \frac{9}{12}, \boxed{\frac{12}{16}}, \boxed{\frac{15}{20}}, \boxed{\frac{18}{24}}$

Rule: Possible answer: Make fractions equivalent to $\frac{3}{4}$ by adding 3 to the numerator and 4 to the denominator.

3. $\frac{1}{5}, \frac{2}{10}, \frac{3}{15}, \boxed{\frac{4}{20}}, \boxed{\frac{5}{25}}, \boxed{\frac{6}{30}}$

Rule: Possible answer: Make fractions equivalent to $\frac{1}{5}$ by adding 1 to the numerator and 5 to the denominator.

4. $\frac{1}{18}, \frac{1}{15}, \frac{1}{12}, \boxed{\frac{1}{9}}, \boxed{\frac{1}{6}}, \boxed{\frac{1}{3}}$

Rule: Possible answer: Subtract 3 from the denominator.

5. $\frac{1}{2}, \frac{1}{4}, \frac{1}{8}, \frac{1}{16}, \boxed{\frac{1}{32}}, \boxed{\frac{1}{64}}, \boxed{\frac{1}{128}}$

Rule: Possible answer: Multiply the denominator by 2.

6. $\frac{1}{3}, \frac{2}{6}, \frac{3}{9}, \frac{4}{12}, \boxed{\frac{5}{15}}, \boxed{\frac{6}{18}}, \boxed{\frac{7}{21}}$

Rule: Possible answer: Make fractions equivalent to $\frac{1}{3}$ by adding 1 to the numerator and 3 to the denominator.

Critical Thinking

Some friends want to share a pizza. Read what they say. Then write the letter of the slice to give each person.

1. "I want $\frac{1}{4}$ of the pizza," said Kate.   B

2. "I want more than Kate," said Miguel.   A

3. "I want half as much as Miguel," said Rosemarie.   E

4. "I want less than Rosemarie," said Joe.   C or D

5. "I want as much as Joe," said Hollis.   D or C

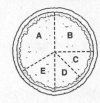

6. Write and illustrate your own pizza problem. Give it to a friend to solve.

Answers will vary. Look for statements that lead to a logical solution.

Visual Thinking

Estimate the fractional part shown by the shading in each picture. Circle the two shapes that show about the same fraction.

Estimates may vary.

1.

$\frac{1}{4}$ $\frac{1}{2}$ $\frac{1}{4}$ $\frac{3}{4}$ 1

2.

$\frac{1}{3}$ $\frac{1}{3}$ $\frac{1}{2}$ $\frac{1}{8}$ $\frac{3}{4}$

3.

$\frac{1}{6}$ $\frac{1}{3}$ $\frac{1}{2}$ $\frac{1}{3}$ $\frac{2}{3}$

4.

$\frac{1}{6}$ $\frac{1}{3}$ $\frac{2}{3}$ $\frac{5}{6}$ $\frac{2}{3}$

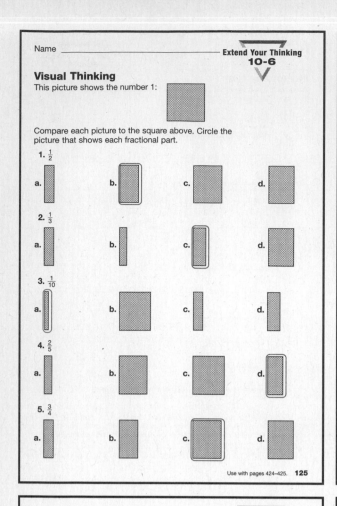

Visual Thinking

This picture shows the number 1:

Compare each picture to the square above. Circle the picture that shows each fractional part.

1. $\frac{1}{2}$

a. b. c. d.

2. $\frac{1}{3}$

a. b. c. d.

3. $\frac{1}{10}$

a. b. c. d.

4. $\frac{2}{5}$

a. b. c. d.

5. $\frac{3}{4}$

a. b. c. d.

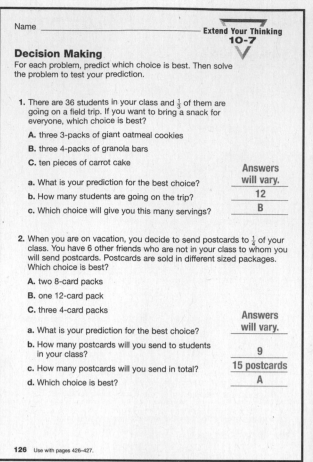

Decision Making

For each problem, predict which choice is best. Then solve the problem to test your prediction.

1. There are 36 students in your class and $\frac{1}{3}$ of them are going on a field trip. If you want to bring a snack for everyone, which choice is best?

    A. three 3-packs of giant oatmeal cookies

    B. three 4-packs of granola bars

    C. ten pieces of carrot cake

    a. What is your prediction for the best choice?   _Answers will vary._

    b. How many students are going on the trip?   _12_

    c. Which choice will give you this many servings?   _B_

2. When you are on vacation, you decide to send postcards to $\frac{1}{4}$ of your class. You have 6 other friends who are not in your class to whom you will send postcards. Postcards are sold in different sized packages. Which choice is best?

    A. two 8-card packs

    B. one 12-card pack

    C. three 4-card packs

    a. What is your prediction for the best choice?   _Answers will vary._

    b. How many postcards will you send to students in your class?   _9_

    c. How many postcards will you send in total?   _15 postcards_

    d. Which choice is best?   _A_

Critical Thinking

Uncle Stan is a food critic for your local newspaper. He eats at restaurants and judges the food. Use his latest Restaurant Ratings to answer each question.

Stan's Restaurant Guide		
Downtown Cosmic Café	$ $ ¢	☆☆
Joe's Grill	$ ¢	☆☆☆ ☆
Daphne's Dinner Emporium	$ $ $	☆
Pierre's House of Crêpes	$ ¢	☆☆
The Koffee Klutch	$	☆☆☆

$ cheap $ $ expensive $ $ $ very expensive
☆ O.K.   ☆☆ good   ☆☆☆ very good

1. Why do some restaurants have half dollar signs or half stars listed after their name?

    Because they lie between one rating and the other; half a symbol means "half–way between."

2. How many dollar signs did Uncle Stan give to the following? Write your answer as a mixed number.

    a. Downtown Cosmic Café $2\frac{1}{2}$

    b. Pierre's House of Crêpes $1\frac{1}{2}$

3. How many stars did Uncle Stan award to the following? Write your answer as a whole or mixed number.

    a. The Koffee Klutch   3

    b. Joe's Grill $2\frac{1}{2}$

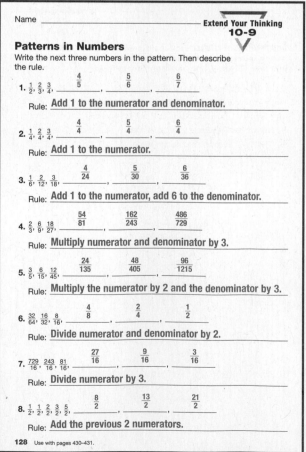

Patterns in Numbers

Write the next three numbers in the pattern. Then describe the rule.

1. $\frac{1}{2}, \frac{2}{3}, \frac{3}{4}$, $\frac{4}{5}$, $\frac{5}{6}$, $\frac{6}{7}$

    Rule: __Add 1 to the numerator and denominator.__

2. $\frac{1}{4}, \frac{2}{4}, \frac{3}{4}$, $\frac{4}{4}$, $\frac{5}{4}$, $\frac{6}{4}$

    Rule: __Add 1 to the numerator.__

3. $\frac{1}{6}, \frac{2}{12}, \frac{3}{18}$, $\frac{4}{24}$, $\frac{5}{30}$, $\frac{6}{36}$

    Rule: __Add 1 to the numerator, add 6 to the denominator.__

4. $\frac{2}{3}, \frac{6}{9}, \frac{18}{27}$, $\frac{54}{81}$, $\frac{162}{243}$, $\frac{486}{729}$

    Rule: __Multiply numerator and denominator by 3.__

5. $\frac{3}{5}, \frac{6}{15}, \frac{12}{45}$, $\frac{24}{135}$, $\frac{48}{405}$, $\frac{96}{1215}$

    Rule: __Multiply the numerator by 2 and the denominator by 3.__

6. $\frac{32}{64}, \frac{16}{32}, \frac{8}{16}$, $\frac{4}{8}$, $\frac{2}{4}$, $\frac{1}{2}$

    Rule: __Divide numerator and denominator by 2.__

7. $\frac{729}{16}, \frac{243}{16}, \frac{81}{16}$, $\frac{27}{16}$, $\frac{9}{16}$, $\frac{3}{16}$

    Rule: __Divide numerator by 3.__

8. $\frac{1}{2}, \frac{1}{2}, \frac{2}{2}, \frac{3}{2}, \frac{5}{2}$, $\frac{8}{2}$, $\frac{13}{2}$, $\frac{21}{2}$

    Rule: __Add the previous 2 numerators.__

Decision Making

There is a big party tonight. You will be in charge of serving the food.

Cut the food pictured below into equal servings to give each person the amount they need. Then explain what you did.

1. There are 21 people at the party. Everyone gets at least 1 piece of pizza. Draw lines to show how you would cut the pizzas.

   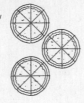

   Explain how you made your decision.

   Student should cut pizzas into at least 21 pieces. Divide total servings needed by pizzas available.

2. There are 18 people at the party. Everyone gets at least 1 piece of corn bread. Draw lines to show how you would cut the bread.

   Explain how you made your decision.

   Student should cut bread into at least 18 pieces. Divide total servings needed by loaves available.

3. There are 10 people at the party. Everyone gets at least 2 pieces of pie. Draw lines to show how you would cut the pies.

   Explain how you made your decision.

   Student should cut pies into at least 20 pieces. Divide total servings needed by pies available.

Visual Thinking

Circle the figure on the right that is the same length as the figure on the left.

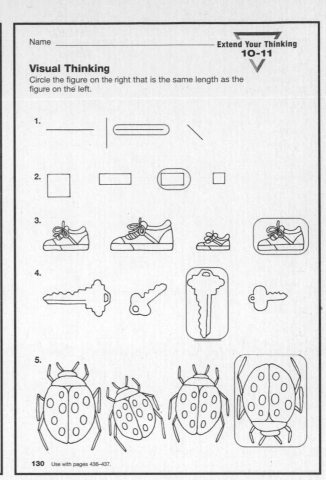

1.

2.

3.

4.

5.

Patterns in Measurement

Use your ruler to measure the length of each item. Write a rule to describe each pattern. Draw the item that would come next.

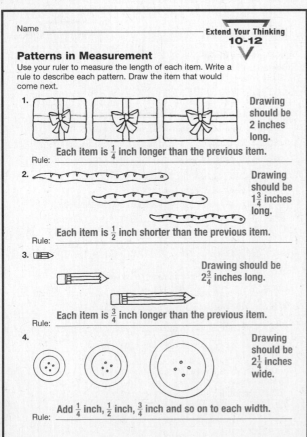

1. Drawing should be 2 inches long.

   Rule: **Each item is $\frac{1}{4}$ inch longer than the previous item.**

2. Drawing should be $1\frac{3}{4}$ inches long.

   Rule: **Each item is $\frac{1}{2}$ inch shorter than the previous item.**

3. Drawing should be $2\frac{3}{4}$ inches long.

   Rule: **Each item is $\frac{3}{4}$ inch longer than the previous item.**

4. Drawing should be $2\frac{1}{4}$ inches wide.

   Rule: **Add $\frac{1}{4}$ inch, $\frac{1}{2}$ inch, $\frac{3}{4}$ inch and so on to each width.**

Critical Thinking

The school librarian just received 27 new books. She needs to put them in a bookcase. To figure out how to arrange the books, she estimated the width of each book.

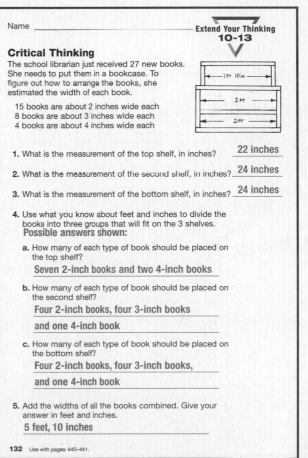

15 books are about 2 inches wide each
8 books are about 3 inches wide each
4 books are about 4 inches wide each

1. What is the measurement of the top shelf, in inches? **22 inches**

2. What is the measurement of the second shelf, in inches? **24 inches**

3. What is the measurement of the bottom shelf, in inches? **24 inches**

4. Use what you know about feet and inches to divide the books into three groups that will fit on the 3 shelves.
   Possible answers shown:

   a. How many of each type of book should be placed on the top shelf?

      Seven 2-inch books and two 4-inch books

   b. How many of each type of book should be placed on the second shelf?

      Four 2-inch books, four 3-inch books and one 4-inch book

   c. How many of each type of book should be placed on the bottom shelf?

      Four 2-inch books, four 3-inch books, and one 4-inch book

5. Add the widths of all the books combined. Give your answer in feet and inches.

   5 feet, 10 inches

Visual Thinking

Suppose you fold a piece of paper in half and then punch holes with a hole punch.

In each row, the drawing on the left shows the paper folded in half. Circle the drawing on the left that shows what the paper will look like when it is unfolded.

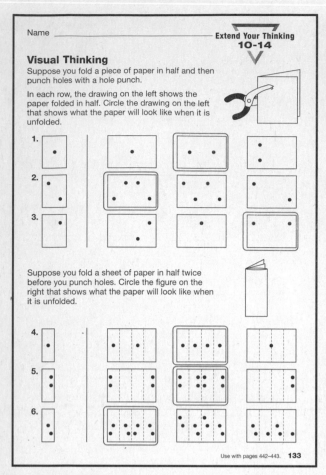

1.
2.
3.

Suppose you fold a sheet of paper in half twice before you punch holes. Circle the figure on the right that shows what the paper will look like when it is unfolded.

4.
5.
6.

Use with pages 442–443. **133**

Decision Making

A soccer club needs to raise money for new uniforms. A survey of how 100 club members want to raise the money shows that 57 would like to have a car wash, 64 would sell magazines, 49 would bake for a bake sale, and 71 would ride in a Bike-a-thon.

1. Complete the bar graph to show this data.

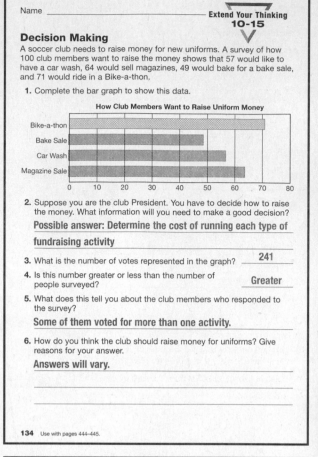

How Club Members Want to Raise Uniform Money

2. Suppose you are the club President. You have to decide how to raise the money. What information will you need to make a good decision?
Possible answer: Determine the cost of running each type of fundraising activity

3. What is the number of votes represented in the graph? **241**

4. Is this number greater or less than the number of people surveyed? **Greater**

5. What does this tell you about the club members who responded to the survey?
Some of them voted for more than one activity.

6. How do you think the club should raise money for uniforms? Give reasons for your answer.
Answers will vary.

134 Use with pages 444–445.

Visual Thinking

Circle the model at the right of the equal sign that shows the answer. Then write the number sentence.

Example

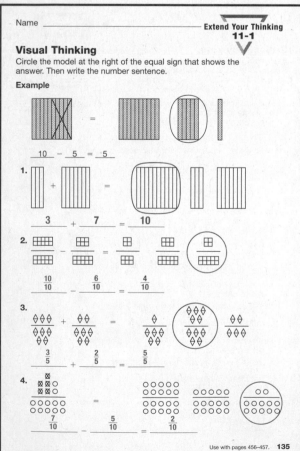

$$\underline{10} - \underline{5} = \underline{5}$$

1.
$$\underline{3} + \underline{7} = \underline{10}$$

2.
$$\frac{10}{10} - \frac{6}{10} = \frac{4}{10}$$

3.
$$\frac{3}{5} + \frac{2}{5} = \frac{5}{5}$$

4.
$$\frac{7}{10} - \frac{5}{10} = \frac{2}{10}$$

Use with pages 456–457. **135**

Critical Thinking

Twelve students in your gym class run a 50-meter race. Here are their times in seconds:

9.90	9.99	8.51	9.09	9.9	8.49
8.5	9.01	8.98	9.11	9.10	9.95

1. Write the times above in order from greatest to least.
9.99, 9.95, 9.90, 9.9, 9.11, 9.10, 9.09, 9.01, 8.98, 8.51, 8.5, 8.49
(Note: the order of 9.90 and 9.9 is interchangeable.)

2. Are there any numbers that are equal? **Yes**
If so, write the equal numbers. **9.90, 9.9**

3. Zachary finished the race first. What was his running time? **8.49**

4. Tad took the greatest amount of time to finish. What was his time?
9.99

5. Charlie finished in fifth place. What was his time? **9.01**

6. Susie finished in eighth place. What was her time? **9.11**

7. Write the finishing times from fastest to slowest.
8.49, 8.5, 8.51, 8.98, 9.01, 9.09, 9.10, 9.11, 9.9, 9.90, 9.95, 9.99

8. Is there a difference between your answer to **1** and your answer to **7**? Explain.
Yes. The fastest time is the least number; From greatest to least is the opposite of from least to greatest.

9. Suppose the third place finisher runs in another race. This time she finishes 0.10 seconds earlier. What was her time in seconds?
8.41 seconds

136 Use with pages 458–459.

**Extend Your Thinking
11-3**

Patterns in Numbers

Write numbers to complete the patterns. Then write the rule you used.

1. 0.1, $\frac{1}{10}$, 0.2, $\frac{2}{10}$, 0.3, $\frac{3}{10}$, __0.4__, __$\frac{4}{10}$__

Rule: **Add 1 tenth. Write each as a decimal, then as a fraction.**

2. 1.2, 1$\frac{3}{10}$, 1.4, 1$\frac{5}{10}$, 1.6, 1$\frac{7}{10}$, __1.8__, __1$\frac{9}{10}$__

Rule: **Add 1 tenth. Alternate writing as a decimal, then as a mixed number.**

3. 3$\frac{1}{10}$, 2.8, 2$\frac{5}{10}$, 2.2, 1$\frac{9}{10}$, 1.6, __1$\frac{3}{10}$__, __1.0__

Rule: **Subtract 3 tenths. Alternate writing as a mixed number, then as a decimal.**

4. four tenths, 0.8, 1$\frac{2}{10}$, one and six tenths, 2.0, 2$\frac{4}{10}$,

two and eight tenths, __3.2__, __3$\frac{6}{10}$__

Rule: **Add 4 tenths. Alternate writing as a word name, then as a decimal, then as a mixed number.**

5. 0.1, $\frac{5}{10}$, 0.9, 1$\frac{3}{10}$, __1.7__, __2$\frac{1}{10}$__, __2.5__, __2$\frac{9}{10}$__

Rule: **Add 4 tenths. Alternate writing as a decimal, then as a fraction or mixed number.**

6. 2$\frac{4}{10}$, 2.1, 1$\frac{8}{10}$, 1.5, __1$\frac{2}{10}$__, __0.9__, __$\frac{6}{10}$__

Rule: **Subtract 3 tenths. Alternate writing as a mixed number or fraction, then as a decimal.**

7. 0.9, 1$\frac{5}{10}$, 2.1, 2$\frac{7}{10}$, 3.3, __3$\frac{9}{10}$__, __4.5__, __5$\frac{1}{10}$__

Rule: **Add 6 tenths. Alternate writing as a decimal, then as a mixed number.**

**Extend Your Thinking
11-4**

Decision Making

You are planning a small party for six people. You will be serving cake and juice. You have $10.00 to spend on party supplies. Here is a list of prices from your local grocery store.

Party Supplies	
12 napkins	$1.13
6 party horns	$2.07
8 large paper plates	$1.77
10 plastic forks	$1.50
1 package of multi-colored streamers	$0.75
6 plastic knives	$1.04
12 plastic spoons	$2.23
Welcome banner	$2.12
8 small paper plates	$0.98
6 party hats	$2.71
8 plastic cups	$1.40
12 multi-colored balloons	$1.39

1. List the supplies that are used for eating and drinking. What is the total cost of these supplies?

Napkins, large paper plates, small paper plates, plastic forks, plastic knives, plastic spoons, plastic cups; Total cost—$10.05

2. List the rest of the supplies in order from most to least expensive. What is the total cost?

Party hats, Welcome banner, party horns, multi-colored balloons, multi-colored streamers; Total cost—$9.04

3. You need to decide which supplies you will buy with $10.00.

a. Do you have enough money to buy all of the supplies on the list?
__No__

b. Write the supplies that you would choose to buy. **Answers may vary. Check that students' choices do not exceed $10.00.**

c. Which supplies did you decide not to buy? Why? **Possible answer: Large paper plates, plastic knives, plastic spoons, party hats, balloons; Because you don't need knives, spoons, and large plates to eat cake, and I didn't have enough money to buy all of the decorating supplies**

**Extend Your Thinking
11-5**

Critical Thinking

Ms. Ortiz's language arts class is performing some scenes from a play. Nick and Anita are in charge of costumes. They need to purchase some fabric, lace, and ribbon. Fabric is sold by the yard; lace and ribbon are sold by the foot.

Here is a list of the items that they would like to purchase:

Item	Cost
5 yards of blue cotton fabric	$1.70 per yard
2 feet of silver sparkle lace	$0.70 per foot
5 feet of white lace ribbon	$0.40 per foot
7 yards of purple felt fabric	$0.70 per yard
2 feet of thin lace	$0.50 per foot
12 feet of satin ribbon	$0.25 per foot
4 yards of white linen fabric	$0.40 per yard

1. How much money will they need to make their purchase?
__$22.40__

2. Describe how you found the total cost.

Possible answer: Multiplied each amount needed by its cost, then added all the products

3. Suppose all the fabric cost $1.05 per yard and all the lace and ribbon cost $0.30 per foot. Find the new total cost. __$23.10__

4. Describe a second way you could solve **3**.

Possible answer: Add the measures of all the fabric and multiply by $1.05. Add the measures of all the lace and ribbon and multiply by $0.30. Add the 2 products.

**Extend Your Thinking
11-6**

Critical Thinking

	Maria's Number Trick	Matt's Number	Ruth's Number
1.	Pick a number from 0 to 10.	7	9
2.	Add 6.	13	15
3.	Subtract the number you picked.	6	6
4.	Add 11.	17	17
5.	Is your sum 17?	yes	yes

1. Try the trick with 2 more numbers. Write the number you choose and the sum. **Chosen numbers may vary, but the final sums should be 17.**

a. Chosen number: _____ **b.** Chosen number: _____

Final sum: _____ Final sum: _____

2. The number you get in step 3 is always added to 11. What number do you have to get in step 3 to get a final sum of 17? __6__

3. Look at steps 1, 2, and 3. Explain why you will always get the same sum in step 3, no matter what number you choose.

Possible answer: First, you add 6 to a number. Then you subtract the same number, so the answer is always 6.

4. Create your own number trick. Make it so that the final result is always the same. Write the steps for your trick below.

Students' math tricks will vary.

_____

_____

Try your trick with two or three numbers to make sure it works. Then try it on a friend.

Visual Thinking

Design a map of your neighborhood. Draw it in the space below. Include buildings, roads, signs, and any rivers or lakes. Label each item with the unit of measurement you would use to measure it. Write cm, m, or km.

Your Home

m

km

Your Road

Answers will vary. Check students' maps for accurate units of measurement.

Patterns in Numbers

What are the next four numbers? Tell what rule was used to make the pattern.

1. 44, 42, 40, 38, __36__ , __34__ , __32__ , __30__
Rule: **Subtract 2.**

2. 3, 6, 12, 24, __48__ , __96__ , __192__ , __384__
Rule: **Multiply by 2.**

3. 1, 4, 9, 16, __25__ , __36__ , __49__ , __64__
Rule: **Multiply 1, 2, 3, . . . 8 by itself.**

4. 13, 20, 27, 34, __41__ , __48__ , __55__ , __62__
Rule: **Add 7.**

5. 4, 20, 100, 500, __2,500__ , __12,500__ , __62,500__
Rule: **Multiply by 5.**

6. 74, 71, 68, 65, __62__ , __59__ , __56__ , __53__
Rule: **Subtract 3.**

7. 2, 4, 8, 16, 32, __64__ , __128__ , __256__
Rule: **Multiply by 2.**

8. 729, 243, 81, __27__ , __9__ , __3__
Rule: **Divide by 3.**

9. 4, 15, 26, 37, __48__ , __59__ , __70__ , __81__
Rule: **Add 11.**

10. 2, 5, 11, 23, __47__ , __95__ , __191__ , __383__
Rule: **Multiply by 2, then add 1.**

Critical Thinking

Some friends want to share a gallon of juice. Read what they say. Then draw a line to the drinking glass to give each person. Do not draw more than one line to any glass.

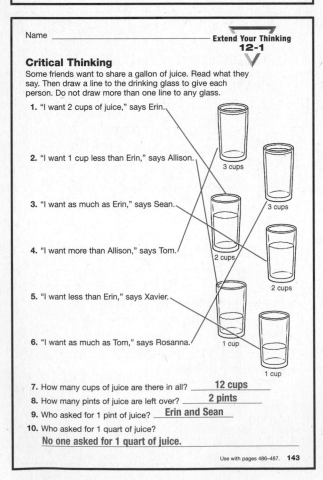

1. "I want 2 cups of juice," says Erin.

2. "I want 1 cup less than Erin," says Allison.

3. "I want as much as Erin," says Sean.

4. "I want more than Allison," says Tom.

5. "I want less than Erin," says Xavier.

6. "I want as much as Tom," says Rosanna.

7. How many cups of juice are there in all? __12 cups__
8. How many pints of juice are left over? __2 pints__
9. Who asked for 1 pint of juice? __Erin and Sean__
10. Who asked for 1 quart of juice?
No one asked for 1 quart of juice.

Visual Thinking

Circle the two shapes in each row with the same area.

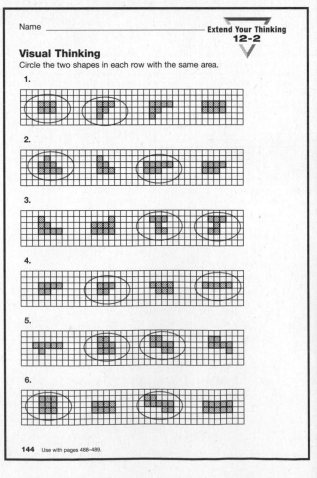

1.

2.

3.

4.

5.

6.

Critical Thinking

Write the correct name under each picture.

1. Max weighs 10 pounds. Kit weighs 3 pounds less than Max. Jake weighs 1 pound more than Kit.

| Max | Jake | Kit |

2. Blanco weighs 5 pounds. Fluffy weighs 16 ounces more than Blanco. Bunny weighs 32 ounces less than Fluffy.

| Fluffy | Bunny | Blanco |

3. Daisy weighs the most. Han weighs 16 ounces less than Daisy. Sunny is the lightest.

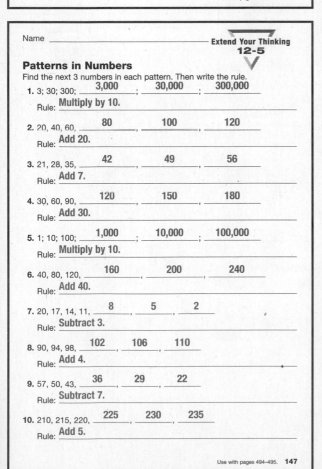

| Han | Daisy | Sunny |

Decision Making

Ms. McGuire is shipping boxes of oranges. She has $52 to spend on shipping. How many of each size box can she send? She wants to send as many oranges as possible.

4 oranges = 1 kg.

An empty box with 24 spaces for oranges = 1 kg.

An empty box with 36 spaces for oranges = 2 kg.

The shipping company charges Ms. McGuire $2 per kilogram to ship the boxes.

1. How many kilograms is a box filled with 24 oranges? **7 kg**

2. How much will Ms. McGuire spend to ship 1 box of 24 oranges? **$14**

3. How many kilograms is a box filled with 36 oranges? **11 kg**

4. How much will Ms. McGuire spend to ship 1 box of 36 oranges? **$22**

5. Make a decision. How many of each size box can Ms. McGuire send? Explain.

Look for solutions that cost $52 or under. Possible answer:

2 boxes of 24 oranges and 1 box of 36 oranges (84 oranges in all) for $50

6. Ms. McGuire also wants to send some packets of dried apricots. 1 packet is 500 g. (Remember: 500 g is half a kg)

a. If she has $3 left, how many packets of apricots could she send?

3 packets

b. If she needs a box that is 500 g when empty, how many packets of apricots could she send?

2 packets

Patterns in Numbers

Find the next 3 numbers in each pattern. Then write the rule.

1. 3; 30; 300; **3,000** ; **30,000** ; **300,000**

Rule: **Multiply by 10.**

2. 20, 40, 60, **80** , **100** , **120**

Rule: **Add 20.**

3. 21, 28, 35, **42** , **49** , **56**

Rule: **Add 7.**

4. 30, 60, 90, **120** , **150** , **180**

Rule: **Add 30.**

5. 1; 10; 100; **1,000** ; **10,000** ; **100,000**

Rule: **Multiply by 10.**

6. 40, 80, 120, **160** , **200** , **240**

Rule: **Add 40.**

7. 20, 17, 14, 11, **8** , **5** , **2**

Rule: **Subtract 3.**

8. 90, 94, 98, **102** , **106** , **110**

Rule: **Add 4.**

9. 57, 50, 43, **36** , **29** , **22**

Rule: **Subtract 7.**

10. 210, 215, 220, **225** , **230** , **235**

Rule: **Add 5.**

Patterns in Numbers

Write the next three measurements.

1. 1 lb, 16 oz, 2 lb, 32 oz, **3 lb** , **48 oz** , **4 lb**

2. 1 L; 1,000 mL; 3 L; 3,000 mL; 5L; **5,000 mL** , **7L** , **7,000 mL**

3. 2 kg; 4 kg; 6,000 g; 8 kg; 10 kg; **12,000 g** , **14 kg** , **16 kg**

4. −15°C, −10°C, −5°C, **0°C** , **5°C** , **10°C**

5. 72°F, 67°F, 62°F, 57°F, **52°F** , **47°F** , **42°F**

6. 8 oz, 1 lb, 24 oz, 2 lb, **40 oz** , **3 lb** , **56 oz**

Complete each pattern.

7. 1 cup, 1 pint, **1 quart** , 2 quarts, 1 gallon, **2 gallons**

8. 20 lb, 17 lb, **14 lb** , 11 lb, **8 lb**

9. 70 g, 700 g, **7 kg** , 70 kg, **700 kg**

10. 0°C, −3°C, **−6°C** , −9°C, **−12°C**

11. 7°F, 14°F, **21°F** , **28°F** , 35°F

12. 8 lb, 4 lb, **2 lb** , **1 lb** , **8 oz** , 4 oz

13. 1 L, 900 mL, **800 mL** , 700 mL, **600 mL**

14. 9 g, 18 g, **27 g** , **36 g** , 45 g

Critical Thinking

Name _____

Extend Your Thinking
12-7

For each picture, decide if it is possible or impossible.

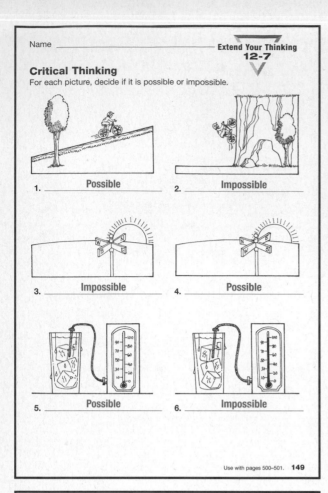

1. __Possible__

2. __Impossible__

3. __Impossible__

4. __Possible__

5. __Possible__

6. __Impossible__

Use with pages 500–501. **149**

Name _____

Extend Your Thinking
12-8

Decision Making

The city of Carsonville has two libraries.

	Main Library	Branch Library
Books	Three floors full of books Some childrens' books Reference room	Limited selection of books Many childrens' books No encyclopedias
Videos	Limited selection Can check out for 3 days	Hundreds of videos Can check out for 1 day
Story Time	Monday–Friday 4:00–5:00	Every Saturday 12:00–2:00

Other information:

The main library is 1 block from a bus stop.
The branch library is 1 mile from a bus stop.
The main library is 2 blocks from the mall.
The branch library is next to a park.

1. Where would you be more likely to find a particular movie?
   __The branch library__

2. Where would you be more likely to find a book about spiders?
   __The main library__

3. Which library offers more hours of story time?
   __The main library__

4. Suppose you are writing a report on Paul Revere. Which library would you choose? Explain your reasoning.
   __Possible answer: The main library; It has a reference room__
   __where I'd be more likely to find information on Paul Revere.__

5. Make a list of reasons why someone might choose the branch library.
   __Possible answers: For the large choice of videos; Because__
   __it's near a park; For the large section of childrens' books;__
   __For story time on Saturdays__

150 Use with pages 502–503.

Name _____

Extend Your Thinking
12-9

Patterns in Data

Look at each group of spinners. Tell what rule was used to make the pattern. Draw the next spinner.

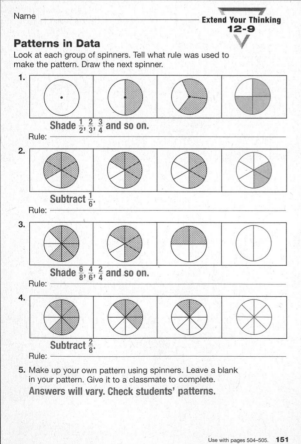

1. Shade $\frac{1}{2}$, $\frac{2}{3}$, $\frac{3}{4}$ and so on.
   Rule: _____

2. Subtract $\frac{1}{6}$.
   Rule: _____

3. Shade $\frac{6}{8}$, $\frac{4}{6}$, $\frac{2}{4}$ and so on.
   Rule: _____

4. Subtract $\frac{2}{8}$.
   Rule: _____

5. Make up your own pattern using spinners. Leave a blank in your pattern. Give it to a classmate to complete.
   Answers will vary. Check students' patterns.

Use with pages 504–505. **151**

Name _____

Extend Your Thinking
12-10

Visual Thinking

Marco and Janine are playing a game using several different spinners. Janine receives points for the spinner landing on a shaded section and Marco receives points for the spinner landing on a white section. The spinners are not fair and Janine is losing! For each question, write the probability that the spinner will land on a shaded spot. Then shade each spinner to make the game fair.

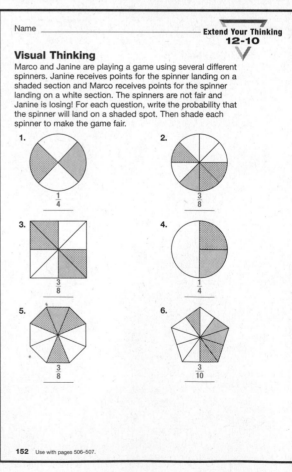

1. $\frac{1}{4}$

2. $\frac{3}{8}$

3. $\frac{3}{8}$

4. $\frac{1}{4}$

5. $\frac{3}{8}$

6. $\frac{3}{10}$

152 Use with pages 506–507.

192

Visual Thinking

Look at each pair of bags. Circle the bag that offers a better chance of choosing a cube.

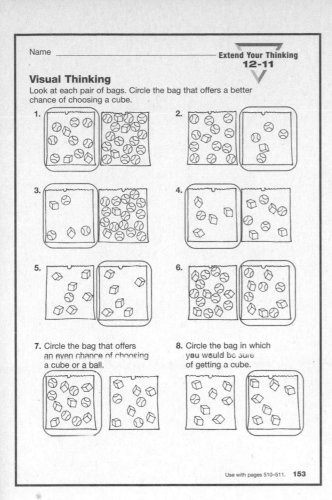

1.

2.

3.

4.

5.

6.

7. Circle the bag that offers an even chance of choosing a cube or a ball.

8. Circle the bag in which you would be sure of getting a cube.